INTERWOVEN DESTINIES

Studies in Judaism and Christianity

Exploration of Issues in the Contemporary Dialogue Between Christians and Jews

Editor in Chief for
Stimulus Books
Helga Croner

Editors
Lawrence Boadt, C.S.P.
Helga Croner
David Dalin
Leon Klenicki
John Koenig
Kevin A. Lynch, C.S.P.
Richard C. Sparks, C.S.P.

 A STIMULUS BOOK

INTERWOVEN DESTINIES

Jews and Christians Through the Ages

edited by
Eugene J. Fisher

A STIMULUS BOOK

PAULIST PRESS ◆ **NEW YORK** ◆ **MAHWAH**

Library of Congress Cataloging-in-Publication Data

Interwoven destinies : Jews and Christians through the ages / edited
  by Eugene J. Fisher.
    p.   cm. — (Studies in Judaism and Christianity) (A Stimulus
  book)
    Includes bibliographical references and index.
    ISBN 0-8091-3363-6
    1. Judaism—Relations—Christianity—History—Congresses.
  2. Christianity and other religions—Judaism—History—Congresses.
  3. Christianity and antisemitism—History—Congresses.   I. Fisher,
  Eugene J.   II. Series.
  BM535b.I493   1993
  261.2'6'09—dc20   92-37707
                                                                CIP

Published by Paulist Press
997 Macarthur Boulevard
Mahwah, N.J. 07430

Printed and bound in the United States of America

Contents

III.
MEDIEVAL DEVELOPMENTS
INSTITUTIONALIZING TENSIONS AND CONFLICTS

IV.
JUDAISM AND CHRISTIANITY
ENTER THE MODERN WORLD

Acknowledgments

The editor would like to acknowledge the efforts of the local organizing committee for the Ninth National Workshop on Christian-Jewish Relations, held in Baltimore, Maryland in May of 1986, for it was in this setting that these papers (with one exception) were first presented. They have been updated by their authors for this publication. Particular gratitude must be given to Charlie and Peggy Obrecht, who have seen to it that the spirit of the National Workshop they so ably hosted has been embodied in an ongoing Institute for Jewish-Christian Studies in Baltimore, and to Dr. James Brashler of St. Mary's University in Baltimore, who began the editing process for this volume.

Dedication

This book is dedicated to the memory of four people whose lives and work greatly influenced the development of the National Workshops and who died in 1992 while this book was under preparation: Rev. John Sheerin of the Paulist Fathers, Rabbi Marc Tanenbaum of the American Jewish Committee, Dr. David Hyatt of the National Conference of Christians and Jews, and Mr. Frank Brennan, founder and editor of *The National Dialogue Newsletter,* an outgrowth of the Workshops. This book too, as always, is an expression of my love for my wife, Cathie, and my daughter, Sarah.

Introduction

Eugene J. Fisher

Out of the maelstrom of events, religious and civil movements, uprisings and tragedies experienced by the Jewish community in the last century of the Second Temple period (i.e., the first of the common era), there emerged intact two Jewish sects whose spiritual insights into the meaning of Jewish history were to affect profoundly the course of the succeeding centuries. The two movements, in a real sense born together out of the rubble of a relatively small temple in a backwater area of the Roman Empire, offered radically different yet strangely similar explanations of the traumatic events of the period, and more, in their youthful exuberance, of the meaning of human history itself.

It is not as if the world took no notice of these events. Indeed, the Romans built perhaps their greatest triumphal arch, which still stands today in Rome, to celebrate the defeat of the Jews and the destruction of the Jerusalem Temple (a triumph they would have to repeat less than a hundred years later). But while the Romans may have felt the matter settled, the two Jewish movements did not. For them, the end of the era of the Second Temple (rebuilt by Jews returning from exile in Babylon centuries earlier after a similar defeat at the hands of a great world empire), was a time not of endings but of beginnings.

The two movements, of course, were rabbinic Judaism and Christianity. Their relationship, like that of many siblings, has always been a difficult one. Yet, as I shall argue and as I think will be seen in the following presentations tracing the relationship, it has also been a remarkably fruitful one, most often in ways neither group has cared to acknowledge. The story that will unfold here is thus one with surprises at every turn. Told and retold (usually by one side or the other, but seldom,

1

as here, by both together), this story has unearthed new facets of discovery—and, yes, of shame, particularly on the side which was to gain the political power with which to enforce its ideas of the "proper" role of the other. One can only speculate how Jews might have used or abused such power over Christians had it been theirs. We shall never know. For only in this generation, two millennia later, has the rebirth of a Jewish state in 'Eretz Israel faced the Jewish people ingathered there with the dilemmas of power. As a Christian, I can only offer the benefit of our own rich and varied experiences over the ages in grappling with it.

The key word to remember in what follows is "surprise." In the last twenty years alone, a tremendous body of literature has arisen from scholars investigating each age of the relationship. Yet almost as fast as theories interpreting the historical and theological meaning of it all have developed, they have had to be abandoned in favor of new theories arising from new insights. Today, we see that no simple theory of the relationship will suffice. We deal here with dynamic realities, with real people, indeed in our post-Second Vatican Council perspective, with a profoundly religious reality, the interaction between two "peoples of God," the church and the Jewish people, or, if you prefer an alternate theory, an ageless interaction within one "people of God," "the children of Abraham."

How Islam, which also claims descent from Abraham, might fit into this picture is a necessary element of the story which will only be hinted at here. This telling will center on the two peoples both claiming continuity with biblical Israel and linked together by common adherence to the same sacred scripture, the Hebrew Bible, which was, in the view of the founders of Christianity and rabbinic Judaism, *the* Bible, God's living and perennial Word to humanity.

A major problem between the two has always been how to *interpret* the scriptures that both hold sacred. The chief interpretative tool for Christianity is embodied in writings set down from the middle to the end of the first century. These writings, which came to be known collectively as the "New" Testament, are considered by Christians equally sacred with the Hebrew scriptures and definitive of their meaning. They center on the story of a Jew, Jesus of Nazareth, claim for him unique authority in defining Jewish tradition, and view the events of his life and his teaching from the perspective of faith in his resurrection from the dead.

As they developed the story of Jesus, the authors of the New Testament, writing some time after his death, and often after the destruction of the Temple in 70 C.E., felt the necessity of accounting for that "other" group of post-destruction Jews who also claimed a definitive interpretation of the Hebrew scriptures for their troubled times. Thus, one finds in the New Testament both a proclamation of faith in Jesus and, at the same time, a polemic against those Jews and that form of Judaism (Pharisaic-rabbinic) which held to its own still developing interpretation.

Fr. Daniel Harrington, S.J., probes what we can know today of Jesus from the historical sources we have. In the process he exposes some of the easy assumptions and misperceptions Christians have harbored in the past concerning the texts themselves and the nature of Judaism in Jesus' time, now revealed as a far more complex and vital community than once we realized. Dr. Michael J. Cook, a Jewish scholar who is also an expert on the New Testament, traces the difficulties modern scholars have had in reconstructing the context out of which the various gospel traditions arose. Our first "surprise," then, is that we know far less than we thought we knew about the formative events of our two traditions, and that much of what we thought we knew, it turns out, was wrong. The fresh insights that emerge from taking Jesus seriously as a Jew of his time, and the New Testament as a product of late Second Temple Judaism, however, offer tremendous potential for understanding both Jesus and his Judaism in richer and deeper ways.

Neither Christianity nor rabbinic Judaism emerged out of the first century as the matured traditions with which we are familiar today. The Nicene Creed, which "centers" all Christian traditions today, was still some three centuries and the work of numerous "Fathers of the Church" away. The Mishnah, the earliest written product of rabbinic Judaism, would not be set down until at least the end of the second century, with the bulk of the Talmud not completed in its present form until much later, in the period which saw the rise and spread of the third Abrahamic faith, Islam.

Modern archaeology and manuscript discoveries, as Professors Martha Himmelfarb and John G. Gager, both of Princeton University, stress, have given us a number of surprises to digest as we tell our own stories of Jewish and Christian history. Judaism, far from being moribund and reduced to the shriveled ghetto-status with which we are familiar from late medieval, western history, remained a major force not only throughout the Roman Empire but outside its boundaries as well. The Jewish communities encountered by developing Christianity were prosperous, vital and very attractive to the very Gentiles whom the Christians (following the apostolic orientation of Paul, Luke and Matthew) sought to convert to the One God, the God of Israel.

One of our most serious and incorrect assumptions concerning the formative centuries of the Jewish-Christian encounter, then, is the notion that the interaction between Jews and Christians was one purely (or even primarily) of hostility on the part of Christians and defensive self-isolation by Jews. Rather, the relationship was far more dynamic on both sides, with much (unacknowledged) sharing of religious insight between the two. It is a dangerous anachronism to project the state of affairs of the late Middle Ages with regard to Christian-Jewish relations back hundreds of years into this period. Chrysostom's fulminations against the synagogue were precipitated by his fear that rabbinic Judaism was becoming *too* attractive to Christians, and as late as the ninth century one can still find bishops complaining that Christians preferred the blessings of rabbis on their homes and fields to the blessings of priests.

Likewise, the legislation of the church, even with the power of the Roman and Byzantine emperors behind it, was still remarkably defensive in character, seeking to limit the attractiveness of Jewish life to Christians, but acknowledging the right of Jews to follow their own traditions and religious practices. This remained true throughout the period when the church's approach to paganism was, simply put, to destroy its temples and convert its followers by any means available. By contrast, forced conversion of Jews (which happened often enough, of course) was officially banned. It was an excommunicable offense throughout the Middle Ages to disrupt Jews at their worship. Jews alone were tolerated within Christian Europe.

By the end of the Middle Ages (12th–16th centuries) however, Jews had been expelled from much of western Europe, and the Jewish community had experienced mass murder at the hands of the Crusaders. In the fourteenth century, passion plays and blood libel charges became popular for the first time and the Jews were even accused of poisoning wells to cause the black death. Both of these latter charges were vigorously condemned by the popes, but by this time, too, the popes themselves had authorized the burning of the Talmud and institutionalized the ghetto and the wearing of distinctive clothing by Jews (Fourth Lateran Council 1213), a particularly obnoxious idea picked up by Christians from Muslim treatment of *both* Jews and Christians.

Clearly, new factors had entered the relationship, and not for the better. Dr. Jeremy Cohen of Ohio State University traces the deteriorating situation, Jewish reactions to it, and offers helpful insights into why it came about. It might be added here that there were doubtlessly external as well as internal reasons for Christendom's increasing intolerance of diversity in its midst. These, I believe, have to do with the rise of Islam and Christianity's perception of it as a mortal threat, a "heresy" capable of consuming the traditions which gave it birth.

Indeed, there was reason for the Crusades. Islam's unprecedented success in sweeping through the ancient Christian communities of Asia Minor and North Africa, up into Spain on the one hand and to the very gates of Vienna on the other, was the major event of the time. Early Islam, too, was remarkably creative both technologically and philosophically, so that the European Renaissance can truly be said to be the result of the clash between Christianity and Islam, with Jews, as it were, caught in the middle, often providing a vital link of communication between the two (as in its crucial role in the development of scholastic philosophy), but also at times being perceived by Christendom as a "fifth column" of potential pro-Muslim sentiment within Christendom itself.

Faced with a serious and highly successful external threat, then, Christianity felt a need for internal cohesiveness. "One society, one religion" and "error has no rights" became rallying cries. In the hardening atmosphere, the anti-Judaic apologetics of the past escalated to a qualitatively new and far more dangerous level. The Inquisition began to view rabbinic Judaism as a heresy from biblical standards, and Jews not simply as a theological remnant of a superseded past, but as a demonic force to be contained and vigorously suppressed. The Spanish "purity of blood" laws presaged the development of modern racism.

Paradoxically, remarkable sharing occurred between the two communities precisely during the periods which saw some of the most oppressive actions of Christian secular and ecclesiastic leaders. Nowhere are the paradoxes more striking than in the Italian peninsula, which gave the very word "ghetto" to our vocabulary. Here, Catholic illuminationists, beautifully and respectfully illustrating Hebrew texts and even prayerbooks, taught generations of Jewish students the best of their art. Synagogues commissioned Catholic composers to set their liturgies to some of the finest music of the Italian Renaissance, and some of the first Talmuds ever to be printed were set by Catholic printing houses in Italy.

Rev. Edward A. Synan of the University of Toronto's Pontifical Institute of Medieval Studies carefully surveys the medieval period, getting beneath our usual historical abstractions to a consideration of the real persons and institutions involved. One late fifteenth-century pope, for example, was capable of heaping indignities on Jews for his own amusement on the one hand, while ensuring on the other that Jews expelled from Spain in 1492 would find safe refuge in the papal states, and imposing *fewer* taxes on them than he did on the Catholic clergy!

Further paradoxical questions thus arise. Leon Poliakov, in the introduction of his three-volume history of antisemitism, asks why, given the negatives of Christianity and Islam toward Judaism, the vast majority of Jews chose to dwell in Christian and Muslim lands. Yosef Yerushalmi, responding to Rosemary Ruether's "straight line" method of historical interpretation which makes no distinction between Nazi antisemitism and New Testament anti-Judaism, said that the real question is not why the medieval church persecuted the Jews, but rather why it allowed them to survive at all in an age when it, as church, did hold the power to "destroy the Jews." Similarly, Dr. Marc Saperstein, in a brilliant introduction to Joshua Trachtenberg's classic, *The Devil and the Jews: The Medieval Conception of the Jews and Its Relations to Modern Antisemitism* (ADL/JPS, 1983) asks how, given Trachtenberg's description, "the Jews were tolerated at all in Christian countries . . . and never made the object of a holy war of extermination?" (p. ix). As Dr. Jaroslav Pelikan of Yale has stated, the "problem of good" may in the long run be even more difficult to comprehend than the "problem of evil."

Dr. Alice Eckardt of Lehigh University examines the attitude toward Jews and Judaism of the great Protestant reformers. She acknowledges with frankness that this was one area of medieval Christianity that the reformers did not critique. Still, she notes, certain aspects of Calvinist appreciation of the Hebrew scriptures offered hope for the future. And the internal and bloody conflicts within divided Christendom would, in later centuries, find a resolution in the concept of separation of church and state, an idea that would also allow Jews a place in societies redefined as religiously "pluralist."

Dr. Arthur Hertzberg shows us the link between the Enlightenment and modern pluralism. He also notes the surprising continuity of so much "enlightened," secular thought on Jews with the high medieval view of society that it fought so bitterly to overturn. Like the medieval and Reformation churches, the Enlightenment was ambivalent about the role and place of Jews in society. Ironically, with the end of a "Christian" society there came not only the end of Christian anti-Judaic theology as a moving principle of social organization, but also the end of that *other* side of Christianity's traditionally ambiguous attitude toward Jews, the side which venerated Judaism as a witness to the validity of the Hebrew scriptures as God's Word, and so legislated the protection of Jewish communities.

While Jews under persecution by the churches (whether Catholic, Protestant or Orthodox), could always convert, there was no escape from modern antisemitism which saw "Jewishness" as an incurable, racially-inherited disease that neither conversion nor assimilation could cure. Through Nazism, modern, racial antisemitism gained the political power to work *its* will on the Jews. For the Nazis there was no question of ghettos, "containment," or even forced conversion. The Jews, for centuries made scapegoats for society's ills and Christian theological insecurities, were fated to die, solely because they *were* Jews.

The Holocaust and the miraculous rebirth of a Jewish state in the land of Israel together demolished any rationale that might have been left for the ancient "teaching of contempt" against Jews and Judaism. The Second Vatican Council, in fact, did no more than officially declare it dead. In 1986, the Bishop of Rome, for the first time since Saint Peter, visited the Great Synagogue of Rome, proclaiming in that act Christian reverence not only for Judaism's Bible, but its acceptance as valid of rabbinic Judaism's *interpretation* of that Bible. After two millennia of apologetics, Christianity today acknowledges that it cannot reflect on the meaning of God's Word for God's people *except* in partnership with the witness and proclamation of the Jewish people. Only together, the church declares, can the witness to God's kingdom be whole.

Today, We Jews and Christians stand on the brink of the third millennium of this ancient interreligious relationship. The contemporary theological implications of this period of "hovering" will be assessed in a second volume—also drawing on the plenary papers of the 1986 National Workshop on Christian-Jewish Relations in Baltimore, as have the papers of the present volume on the history of Jewish-Christian relations.

I.
CHRISTIANITY IN THE CONTEXT OF SECOND TEMPLE JUDAISM

The Teaching of Jesus in His Context

Daniel J. Harrington, S.J.

The overall theme of the Ninth National Workshop on Christian-Jewish Relations is summarized in the expression, "Coming to Grips With Our Past: Forging Our Future." This theme suggests that by better understanding what has happened between Christians and Jews in the past, we will be better able to work out our future together. The program before us promises to take us through the history of our relationship up to the present day. It is a privilege to be part of such a fascinating and ambitious project.

It is only appropriate that the very first topic on our agenda should be the teaching of Jesus in his context. One of the most encouraging developments between Jews and Christians in recent years has been a shared interest in the person of Jesus. Some Jewish scholars have engaged in the task of "bringing Jesus home" to Judaism; that is, in studying the Jewish context of Jesus' life and teaching and in pointing out the positive attitude toward Jesus that Jews today might have.[1] Other Jewish historians have worked at clarifying the precise kind of Judaism that Jesus represented and in showing his continuity with the Jewish tradition.[2]

On the other hand, Christian historians have taken up the challenge of interpreting Jesus and his teachings in the context of Judaism during the first century and in the land of Israel.[3] Theologians have welcomed this emphasis on the Jewishness of Jesus precisely because it stresses his humanity and defends against Christianity's long-time temptation toward docetism (the heresy that maintains that Jesus was a divine being who *only appeared* to be human).

The context of Jesus' teaching was Judaism. To be even more precise, its context was first-century Judaism in the land of Israel. Thus there is a basic level on which Christians and Jews can agree about Jesus of Nazareth. That Jesus the Galilean was born, lived, and died in the land of Israel in the early part of what we now call the first century C.E. cannot be doubted. This Jesus was a Jewish teacher, though of a somewhat unusual type. He taught by means of short sayings and parables, which could be easily remembered and then recited from memory. He attracted disciples, who came to learn from him and to be with him. While Capernaum may have been his base of operations, much of his teaching ministry involved traveling from place to place and relying on the hospitality of local people. His first followers were encouraged to share his itinerant ministry of preaching God's kingdom and healing the sick.

Much of his teaching recorded in the gospels breathes the air of first-century Judaism. Though now expressed in Greek, those teachings incorporate Semitic idioms and words, presuppose conditions that prevailed in the land of Israel, and respond well to translation back into Aramaic or Hebrew. Jesus seems to have taught in Aramaic, though like other Jews of his day he knew Hebrew, may well have spoken some Greek, and had exposure to Latin. As he taught various audiences in Galilee, he readily appealed to their familiarity with sowing seeds (see Mk 4:3–9, 26–29, 30–32), baking bread (see Mt 13:33), hiding treasure (see Mt 13:44), fishing (see Mt 13:47–50), and so forth. All these activities were so familiar to Jesus' audiences in the land of Israel during the first century that they needed no explanation.[4] By appealing to the everyday experiences of his audiences, Jesus was able to lead them to further reflection on the person of God, the kingdom of God, and God's dealings with his people.

The content of Jesus' teaching is firmly rooted in Judaism as it is expressed in the Hebrew Bible and the Jewish tradition. The God of Jesus can be approached as a loving Father. This God created and sustains all things. This God has entered into a special relationship with the people of Abraham, Isaac, and Jacob. This God has special concern for the poor and the outcast. There is no doubt: The God of Jesus is Israel's God.

Along with other Jews of his day, Jesus looked to the time when God would intervene in his people's history and when all creation would acknowledge the sovereignty of God. This decisive moment in human history, or rather the end of human history as we know it, is what is meant by the expression "the kingdom of God." Preparation for God's kingdom requires repentance and constant vigilance. Not all Jews in the land of Israel at Jesus' time necessarily shared this sharp sense of God's imminent intervention. Moreover, Jesus himself seems to have been concerned with showing how God's kingdom was already inaugurated and with tempering speculations about the precise time of the kingdom's arrival. Nevertheless, it remains clear that the phrase that summarizes Jesus' teaching is the line from his own prayer: "Thy kingdom come" (see Mt 6:10; Lk 11:2).

The context of Jesus' teaching was Judaism in the land of Israel in the first century. Jesus was a Jewish teacher. He spoke Aramaic, used the methods of Jewish teachers of his day, and spoke basically to other Jews. His teachings about God, God's kingdom, and God's dealings with his people were thoroughly Jewish. About such matters, Jewish and Christian scholars can agree.

The new spirit of cooperation between Jewish and Christian scholars has led to even further clarifications about the Jewish context of Jesus' teaching. Two examples will have to suffice here. The first concerns the nature of Jesus' opponents. In the first three gospels (Matthew, Mark, and Luke), the usual opponents of Jesus throughout his teaching career are the Pharisees. They show up in the strangest places and contexts—from Galilean grain fields (see Mk 2:24) to the Temple area (see Mk 12:13), though once the passion narrative begins they drop out of sight. The gospel of John lumps the Jewish opponents of Jesus under the general term *hoi Ioudaioi,* which means "the Judeans" or "the Jews." What both Jewish and Christian scholars have recognized more clearly in recent years, is that these generally negative characterizations of Jesus' opponents probably say more about the evangelists than about Jesus. In the period when the gospels were written—after 70 c.e.; that is, after the Roman capture of the Jerusalem Temple, Christians and Jews alike were trying to reconstruct their Judaism now without the Temple, and in a real sense without possession of their land. In their efforts to distinguish the Christian communities from the Jewish synagogues, and perhaps in response to provocations from those synagogues, the evangelists placed even greater emphasis than Jesus or their traditions did on the Pharisees or "the Jews" as the opponents of Jesus. Thus their negative portraits probably say more about conditions after 70 c.e. than they do about the context of Jesus' teaching.[5]

A second example concerns the responsibility for Jesus' death. The trial and death of Jesus have been discussed extensively by Jews and Christians during the last thirty years. There is fundamental agreement that the ultimate legal responsibility for Jesus' death lay with the Roman

governor, Pontius Pilate. Jesus was executed as a perceived political
threat ("the King of the Jews") to the Roman establishment and according to a Roman method of punishment (crucifixion). There is also fundamental agreement that the evangelists deliberately played down Roman
responsibility and emphasized Jewish involvement for Jesus' death. The
degree of Jewish involvement in the events leading up to Jesus' death is
still disputed. There is, of course, no basis for thinking that all the Jewish
people in the land of Israel in the first century consented to Jesus'
condemnation and execution. Still less is there any question of inherited
responsibility. What remains disputed is this: Were the Jewish elders and
chief priests in Jerusalem unwilling agents, passive spectators, active
collaborators, or the initiators in the process that led to Jesus' condemnation and execution?[6]

In the first part of my presentation, I have sketched areas of general
agreement about the Jewish context of Jesus' teaching. Both the methods and the contents of Jesus' teaching fit Judaism in the land of Israel
during the first century. The Jewish opposition to Jesus the Jew was
probably more diffuse and less strident than the four gospels indicate.
Whatever Jewish opposition Jesus may have stirred up, the final responsibility for his death lay with Pontius Pilate.

The second part of my presentation will focus on three problems
involved in talking about the Jewish context of Jesus' teaching: the diverse nature of Judaism in Jesus' time, the limitations imposed by our
ancient sources about Jesus, and the difference in our theological assessments of Jesus.[7] In raising these issues, I play the role neither of apologist nor of conciliator. Rather I raise them, because by coming to grips
with these issues, Christians and Jews may be in a better position to
forge their common future. They represent our common scholarly
agenda and demand our cooperation. By working together on them, we
may come to know one another better and to respect one another more
deeply.

The first problem area concerns the nature of Judaism in Jesus'
time. Two questions can reveal what is at stake here: What kind of Jew
was Jesus? Against the background of what corpus of literature or what
Jewish movement should we interpret Jesus' teaching?

We will address the second question first: Against which Jewish
background should we interpret Jesus' teaching? There was a time not
too long ago when scholars worked on the basis of clear and uncomplicated assumptions about Judaism in the land of Israel in the first century.
There were Pharisees and Sadducees, something like Democrats and

Republicans in America today. Off by the side were the so-called "people of the land," the shadowy Essenes, the elusive Zealots, and wild apocalyptists.

This simple picture of first-century Judaism was shattered by the discovery of the Dead Sea scrolls in the late 1940s and early 1950s.[8] The caves at Qumran yielded manuscripts of the Hebrew Bible a thousand years older than what was previously available, versions of ancient Jewish Pseudepigrapha (some previously unknown), and documents that illuminated the life of the Qumran sect. Very early in the scholarly debate, the Qumran group was identified as an Essene community. It apparently lived a patterned life of monastic isolation and prepared itself for vindication in the coming of God's kingdom. Now we had the library of a Jewish sect from Jesus' time.

The discovery of the Dead Sea scrolls has led to a thoroughgoing reassessment of other Jewish writings. New editions and translations of the Apocrypha and Pseudepigrapha have appeared, with competent and reliable new handbooks to aid in their interpretation.[9] Some scholars argued that the Targums, the Aramaic translations/paraphrases of the Hebrew Bible, represented the liturgical life of Jews at the turn of the era and so could be used in interpreting the New Testament.[10] The Mishnah has been restudied in the historical setting of its final editing around 200 C.E. The result has been greater caution about retrojecting material in the Mishnah into the first century and greater appreciation of the creativity and coherent program of the Mishnah's architects.[11]

What emerges from this great burst of scholarly activity is the conviction that Judaism in Jesus' time was quite diverse. There were many varieties of Judaism—so many that we can hardly speak of a mainstream or normative Judaism anymore. The most obvious rallying points for the various types of Judaism are the Jerusalem Temple, the Torah, and the land of Israel. But even here there is hesitation on the part of some scholars to view any or all of these as the core or center of Judaism in the first century. The archaeologists have confirmed this impression of variety in first-century Judaism with their evidence for regionalism not only among Galilee, Samaria, and Judea but even within parts of Galilee.[12] The old, uncomplicated picture of first-century Judaism has been destroyed. Its place has been taken by a more complex and variegated model, which has ramifications for the context of Jesus' teaching.

So we return to our first question: What kind of Jew was Jesus? There was a time when one could assume that the rabbinic writings provided the background for Jesus' teaching. Now there are more varied resources available and some doubt as to how far back the rabbinic writings go.

This development in our understanding of first-century Judaism manifests itself in various approaches to the identity and background of Jesus. In recent years, Jesus has been portrayed as an eschatological prophet against the background of Jewish apocalyptic writings, a political revolutionary against the background of Josephus' reports about rebels against Rome, an Essene against the background of the Dead Sea scrolls, a Galilean charismatic against the background of rabbinic accounts about Galilean holy men, a Hillelite against the background of the Hillel-Shammai debates, and a Galilean rabbi against the background of the Targums. The list could go on. The point is that our increased appreciation of the variety represented in first-century Judaism makes it even harder to know precisely what kind of Jew Jesus was and against which background he should be interpreted.

The second problem involved in placing Jesus' teaching in its context concerns the nature of the ancient sources about it. There is not much on the Jewish side. The Toledot Jeshu tradition and the few talmudic passages about Jesus are fascinating examples of religious polemic and parody but tell us practically nothing about Jesus. The so-called Testimonium Flavianum in Josephus' *Jewish Antiquities* 18:63–64 has been variously interpreted as wholly spurious, wholly authentic, or somewhere in between. At least some parts of it ("he was the messiah . . . on the third day he appeared to them, restored to life") sound like statements made by a Christian writer or editor.[13]

The most extensive and important ancient sources about Jesus are the four gospels. They describe the life, teaching, and death of Jesus in the land of Israel in the early first century C.E. Yet they seem to have been composed only after 70 C.E., in the late first century. They presupposed the Easter event. They worked on two levels: While describing Jesus around 30 C.E., they also addressed Christian communities in the late first century and outside of the land of Israel. Between Jesus and the evangelists there was a complicated and probably unsystematic process of the transmission of traditions about Jesus. The earliest Christians were more concerned with proclaiming Jesus than writing books.

Some modern students of the gospels have tried to get behind the texts of the four gospels to the original teachings of the historical Jesus. Christian scholars often rely on the so-called criterion of dissimilarity or discontinuity. According to this criterion, a teaching that has no (or little) parallel in Jewish or early Christian writings can be safely traced back to the earthly Jesus.[14] The obvious problem with this criterion of dissimilarity or discontinuity is that it takes Jesus and his teachings out of their Jewish context entirely, or at least suggests that the teachings shared by Jesus with other Jewish teachers are uninteresting or unimportant.

Jewish students of the gospels often practice the reverse type of criticism by applying what can be called the criterion of similarity or continuity. They assume that Jesus is to be understood solely within the framework of first-century Judaism as they perceive it. Whatever does not fit their perception of Judaism is assigned to the evangelists, or to the early church, or to the peculiarities of Jesus himself. This approach to the Jewish context of Jesus' teaching was summarized many years ago by Claude G. Montefiore: "His teaching, where good, was not original, and where original was not Jewish or good."[15]

Thus the gospels are not easy sources to use if we wish to gain further illumination about the context of Jesus' teaching. The criterion of dissimilarity/discontinuity wrenches Jesus' teaching out of its Jewish context. The criterion of similarity/continuity leaves it within the boundaries of Judaism and dismisses what does not fit as uninteresting, unimportant, or eccentric.

The third problem involved in dealing with the Jewish context of Jesus' teaching concerns our differing theological assessments of Jesus. The gospels portray Jesus not only as a great Jewish teacher about God and the human condition, but also as the decisive revelation of God, the one who brought to fulfillment the revelations previously accorded to the people of God. Much of Jesus' teaching stands within the boundaries of the Torah and the Jewish wisdom tradition. Yet at some points, Jesus appears to go beyond these traditions and to function as their authoritative interpreter who can bypass or even abrogate the Torah. Rather than presenting Jesus as standing under the Torah, the gospels picture Jesus as standing over the law and treat it with reference to Jesus.

The six antitheses in the Sermon on the Mount illustrate this idea. In some instances in Matthew 5:21–48, Jesus goes behind a biblical prohibition (against murder and adultery) to get to the root disposition (anger and lust). But his teaching on divorce ("everyone who divorces his wife, except on the ground of unchastity, makes her an adulteress; and whoever marries a divorced woman commits adultery," Mt 5:32) bypasses and even abrogates the permission granted to the husband to divorce his wife by Deuteronomy 24:1. Jesus' statement on not swearing oaths at all goes far beyond the biblical prohibition against swearing falsely (see Lev 19:12; Num 30:2; Deut 23:21). His teaching about forgoing retaliation pushes the biblical *lex talionis* (see Ex 21:23–24; Lev 24:19–20; Deut 19:21) to the point of abrogation.

A similar theological difference emerges from reflection on the significance of Jesus' death. Jews and Christians alike can look upon Jesus as another victim of outside oppression. Thus they can situate his execution under Pontius Pilate in the context of other religious-political martyrs throughout Jewish and Christian history. This approach to Jesus as suffering just one and martyr is deeply rooted in Jewish tradition and can be a fruitful source of theological reflection among Jews and Gentiles even in our own day, perhaps especially so in the light of Hitler's Holocaust.

Nevertheless, we can walk along this path only part of the way. The gospels and the other New Testament writings go beyond this suffering just one/martyr Christology. They portray Jesus' death as bringing salvation to the whole world. They attribute his death not only to human agents (Pilate, Judas, Jewish leaders) but also to God's will and plan for humanity's salvation. Terms such as redemption, reconciliation, justification, atonement, and so forth, express what has taken place as the result of Jesus' death, according to Christian faith.

In the last analysis, Jews and Christians draw different theological conclusions about Jesus the teacher and Jesus the victim. Christians believe that Jesus the Jewish teacher was God's definitive interpretation of the Torah and that his suffering brought about a new relationship between God and humanity.

Jews and Christians should welcome the recent attention given to the Jewish context of Jesus' teaching as a help to mutual understanding and religious cooperation. But it is important for us to come to grips with some problems involved in talking about the Jewishness of Jesus: (1) Our increased understanding of the diversity within Palestinian Judaism in Jesus' time makes it difficult to know precisely what kind of Jew Jesus was and against which background we should try to interpret him; (2) Jewish sources about Jesus are either late or suspect; Christian sources have passed through a complicated process of tradition. Those who try to get behind the sources either take Jesus out of Judaism or interpret him entirely within Judaism; (3) Both Jews and Christians view Jesus as a teacher and a victim of oppression. However, their ultimate theological assessments of Jesus differ.

In clarifying these three problems, I have tried to be neither conciliator nor apologist. Rather, I have sought to make clear the three methodological issues that Christians and Jews confront together: the complex character of Second Temple Judaism, the nature of our ancient sources about Jesus, and the different theological perspectives that we bring to these sources about Jesus.

The recognition of our differences about Jesus does not mean that we cannot work together; in fact, it demands that we do so. And we are working together. Jewish and Christian scholars routinely collaborate in studying Second Temple Judaism, interpreting the gospels, and determining the significance of Jesus the Jew. Their collaborative efforts provide us with a good example of our conference theme: "Coming to Grips with Our Past: Forging Our Future." By facing together our common problems about placing Jesus the Jew in his historical context, I am confident that we will be better able to work out our future together.

NOTES

1. See S. Ben Chorin, *Bruder Jesus: Der Nazarener in jüdischer Sicht* (3rd ed., Munich: List, 1970). For a full discussion from an evangelical perspective, see D. A. Hagner, *The Jewish Reclamation of Jesus: An Analysis and Critique of Modern Jewish Study of Jesus* (Grand Rapids: Zondervan, 1984).

2. G. Vermes, *Jesus the Jew. A Historian's Reading of the Gospels* (rev. ed., Philadelphia: Fortress, 1981); *Jesus and the World of Judaism* (Philadelphia: Fortress, 1984).

3. A. E. Harvey, *Jesus and the Constraints of History* (Philadelphia: Westminster, 1982); M. Hengel, *The Charismatic Leader and His Followers* (New York: Crossroad, 1981); C. Perrot, *Jésus et l'histoire* (Tournai: Desclée, 1979); J. Riches, *Jesus and the Transformation of Judaism* (London: Darton, Longman & Todd, 1980); E. P. Sanders, *Jesus and Judaism* (Philadelphia: Fortress, 1985).

4. J. Jeremias, *The Parables of Jesus* (rev. ed., New York: Scribners, 1963).

5. See M. J. Cook, *Mark's Treatment of the Jewish Leaders* (Leiden: Brill, 1978); J. L. Martyn, *History and Theology in the Fourth Gospel* (2nd rev. ed., Nashville: Abingdon, 1979).

6. See J. Blinzler, *The Trial of Jesus* (Westminster, MD: Newman, 1959); S. F. G. Brandon, *The Trial of Jesus of Nazareth* (New York: Stein & Day, 1968); R. Gordis (ed.), *The Trial of Jesus in the Light of History*, in *Judaism* 20 (1971) 6–74; E. Rivkin, *What Crucified Jesus?* (Nashville: Abingdon, 1984); G. S. Sloyan, *Jesus on Trial* (Philadelphia: Fortress, 1973); W. R. Wilson, *The Execution of Jesus* (New York: Scribner's, 1970); and P. Winter, *On the Trial of Jesus* (Berlin: de Gruyter, 1961).

7. A fuller treatment of these issues (with extensive bibliography) appears in my article, "The Jewishness of Jesus: Facing Some Problems," *Catholic Biblical Quarterly* 49 (1987).

8. G. Vermes, *The Dead Sea Scrolls. Qumran in Perspective* (Cleveland:

Collins & World, 1978). For more recent publications, see C. Koester, "A Qumran Bibliography: 1974–1984," *BTB* 15 (1985) 110–20.

9. J. H. Charlesworth (ed.), *The Old Testament Pseudepigrapha* (2 vols., Garden City, NY: Doubleday, 1983, 1985); H. F. D. Sparks (ed.), *The Apocryphal Old Testament* (New York: Clarendon Press, Oxford, 1984). For a general introduction to this literature and the Qumran writings, see M. E. Stone (ed.), *Jewish Writings of the Second Temple Period* (Philadelphia: Fortress, 1984).

10. R. Le Déaut, *The Message of the New Testament and the Aramaic Bible* (Rome: Biblical Institute Press, 1982).

11. J. Neusner, *Judaism: The Evidence of the Mishnah* (Chicago-London: University of Chicago Press, 1981).

12. See E. M. Meyers and J. F. Strange, *Archaeology, the Rabbis, and Early Christianity: The Social and Historical Setting of Palestinian Judaism and Christianity* (Nashville: Abingdon, 1981).

13. For a survey of scholarship, see L. H. Feldman, *Josephus and Modern Scholarship (1937–1980)* (Berlin-New York: de Gruyter, 1984) 679–703.

14. Good examples of the application of these criteria are found in N. Perrin, *Rediscovering the Teaching of Jesus* (New York-Evanston, IL: Harper & Row, 1967).

15. C. G. Montefiore, "Jewish Conceptions of Christianity," *Hibbert Journal* 28 (1929–1930) 249.

Turning the Corner in Dialogue: A Jewish Approach to Early Christian Writings

Michael J. Cook

It actually happened about fifty years ago, when a traveling circus came to Brooklyn, that one evening a lion broke loose from his cage. No sooner was the escape discovered than the search was on! At dawn, the keepers located him. Strangely enough, he had gone but several blocks, stopping at an abandoned house with a thirty-foot strand of fence in front of it. There was the lion, pacing back and forth before that fence, continuing that same monotonous yet comfortable habit of *lateral* movement into which he had been born in a circus cage, free—and yet at the same time not entirely free after all. For whenever he reached a corner, at one end of the fence, he simply reversed his direction. Having broken out of one cage, he had become complacent with yet another, and simply could not bring himself to turn that corner![1]

It was likewise a number of decades ago that we Christians and Jews broke out of our own patterns of enshacklement vis-à-vis one another, leaving them, so we may think, far behind us. We have witnessed in recent years how far our scholars and clergy have traveled along avenues of new understanding, especially on the theme of the New Testament in relation to its Jewish context. But have we truly made good our escape from our former chains? Frankly, I think not! For I fear that we have been producing activities faster than progress and mistaking *lateral* movement for *forward* marching.

I enthusiastically endorse our proliferation of academic symposia and clergy institutes; they are absolutely essential. Yet our programming

21

on the New Testament may have become essentially only replication. Reminiscent of the lion, we are engaged in lateral pacing before a fence whose corners we are afraid to turn, corners concerning which there is no getting around that we are not getting around. Because I consider this fence a barrier of such consequence, addressing it head-on becomes integral to this essay.

I have participated as a speaker in well over two hundred Jewish-Christian academic and clergy symposia on the New Testament. Yet most of these have been adjourned with a tacit acknowledgment that the material discussed was never going to be genuinely communicated by the participants to their respective laities. Somehow our churchgoers and synagoguegoers do not really receive the substantive learning and understanding these conferences engender. As I shall explain shortly, by "substance" I mean knowledge sufficient to comprehend those dynamics of the New Testament's development that impinge, in fundamental ways, on Jewish-Christian relations today.

One reason for the general hesitance to bring our laities into such participation falls under the rubric of *benign elitism*. Many academicians and clergy feel that, when it comes to study of the New Testament, most laypersons are simply lacking in the skills, training, and interest requisite for their assimilating in depth what for academicians, clergy, and seminarians are, after all, areas of expertise and full-time commitment. The scientific study of the New Testament and the quest for the historical Jesus are held to be properly the domains of the experts only.

Reinforcing this hesitance is a sense of *futility*. The laity, it is often felt, are governed by deep-seated preconceptions. It would be counterproductive to attempt change among those deemed entirely resistant to change. Thus, for instance, rabbis know that many Jews cringe upon hearing the name of Jesus, this a product of centuries of persecution of Jews, often perpetrated in Jesus' name, and frequently underpinned by recourse to anti-Jewish citations from the New Testament. In Dayton, Ohio, for example, when a rabbi helping children learn their Hebrew names explained that the Hebrew name for Joshua, "Yehoshua," was also the Hebrew name for Jesus, one little girl covered her ears while exclaiming, "I don't want to ever hear that name! It gives me the shivers!" Her comment most likely reflected a type of deep-seated family attitude which rabbis may feel it futile ever to try to undo.

So, too, it is argued in a different vein, are Christian laypersons firm in their preconceptions and misconceptions. Here the influence of the

New Testament's anti-Jewish stereotyping is commonly presumed indelible, suggesting in turn that attempts to tamper with what is tamper-proof may be doomed to failure. Thus, while Christian and Jewish clergy and scholars can learn from one another, the problems of effecting change within the *lay* arena might just as well be left alone!

Paradoxically, fear of *successful* communicating may constitute a third excuse for not tackling this problem. I have encountered such apprehension among some colleagues in the Christian clergy, as well as among some Christian seminarians I have taught. They are fearful lest they undermine their own laity's confidence in the New Testament. So many of the Christian laity, it is held, consider the New Testament to be sacred, if not infallible, in every word, reminiscent of that commonly spotted or sported bumper sticker: "Jesus said it! I believe it! And that settles it!" They are alleged to be simply not ready for exposure to the views of scholars and clergy who acknowledge that not all gospel statements necessarily represent the "gospel truth!"

Many Christian clergy have learned in their own seminaries that those New Testament traditions most responsible for spawning ill-will between Christians and Jews do not genuinely go back to the historical Jesus. Yet they do not see how they can communicate the results of literary, form, and redaction criticism to congregants resistant to the idea that only *some* of the gospels' teachings go back to Jesus, while others reflect later developments retrojected to him. Would not such disclosure damage their people's confidence respecting the remainder of the New Testament? Once the whittling process begins, where would it end up? And how would the laity then view their clergy and educators from whom they expect full commitment (albeit defining "commitment" in a narrow kind of way)?

This, then, is the fence whose corners I submit we Jews and we Christians are hesitant to turn. Our multiplication of symposia is of such a nature as to allow us to sidestep what we most urgently need to be doing—generating forward progress rather than intensifying lateral movement, addressing the reality that what academicians teach and many clergy know the laity rarely know or hear or have opportunity to learn.

How have we allowed ourselves to forget that the history of Jewish-Christian relations has not been the history of relations between Jewish and Christian scholars nor that between Jewish and Christian theologians or clergy? But it has been the history of relations between synagoguegoers and churchgoers, between Jewish laypersons and Christian laypersons. Throughout our trouble-ridden history with one another, it has been within the wider lay social contexts (neighborhood living, business interaction, public and private school education as well as education in one's own houses of worship) that bias, suspicion, stereotyping, and misunderstanding have assumed deep roots, becoming virtually independent from and impervious to whatever shifts in attitude or policy may eventuate within clerical or academic circles. Since, unless they are taught otherwise, most laity automatically incline toward acceptance of biblical texts at face value, it is primarily among our lay constituents that we still encounter those uncritical and literalist comprehensions of the biblical message which for centuries have fueled divisiveness and ill-will between Christian and Jew. If the ultimate goals of academic/clergy symposia do not include intentions to implement changes within the lay arena, then I submit we are only going through our lateral paces.

I therefore propose that we designate the next twenty years as a reasonable time frame for turning these corners of incomprehension and, as an aid to our resumption of this kind of forward progress, I also propose that *five specific perspectives* be incorporated into our lay education projects (whether in the church and synagogue arena or the university classroom). I am less concerned with laypersons *accepting* these perspectives than I am with their merely having *exposure* to them. Accordingly, it may be preferable to view these five perspectives as only "working hypotheses." I am also open to the possibility that these working hypotheses may not "work"! Indeed, I shall include below, where appropriate, some of my own critique of these approaches. Nonetheless, since these perspectives do reflect the contours of a sufficiently recognizable pattern of Jewish scholarly endeavor on the New Testament,[2] they serve an important function in Jewish-Christian dialogue, constituting approaches with which Jewish and Christian laypersons, not to mention clergy and academicians, should become adequately conversant.

PERSPECTIVE #1

The *first* perspective proceeds from the observation that the gospels' Jesus does not speak in a consistent voice about his fellow Jews or Judaism. Thus, while presented in some passages as urging the love of peace and the turning of the other cheek, elsewhere, when addressing fellow Jews, Jesus is vindictive and vitriolic. How are laypersons, Christian or Jewish, to reconcile the Jesus who says that ". . . every one who is [even] angry with his brother shall be liable to judgment" (Mt 5:22),

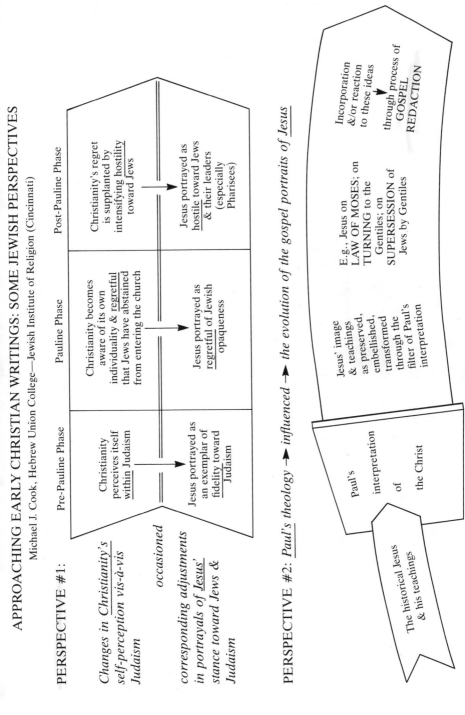

APPROACHING EARLY CHRISTIAN WRITINGS: SOME JEWISH PERSPECTIVES

Michael J. Cook, Hebrew Union College—Jewish Institute of Religion (Cincinnati)

PERSPECTIVE #1:

Changes in Christianity's self-perception vis-à-vis Judaism

occasioned

corresponding adjustments in portrayals of Jesus' stance toward Jews & Judaism

Pre-Pauline Phase | Pauline Phase | Post-Pauline Phase

Christianity perceives itself within Judaism → Jesus portrayed as an exemplar of fidelity toward Judaism

Christianity becomes aware of its own individuality & regretful that Jews have abstained from entering the church → Jesus portrayed as regretful of Jewish opaqueness

Christianity's regret is supplanted by intensifying hostility toward Jews → Jesus portrayed as hostile toward Jews & their leaders (especially Pharisees)

PERSPECTIVE #2: *Paul's theology* → *influenced* → *the evolution of the gospel portraits of Jesus*

The historical Jesus & his teachings

Paul's interpretation of the Christ

Jesus' image & teachings as preserved, embellished, transformed through the filter of Paul's interpretation

E.g., Jesus on LAW OF MOSES; on TURNING to the Gentiles; on SUPERSESSION of Jews by Gentiles

Incorporation &/or reaction to these ideas through process of GOSPEL REDACTION

PERSPECTIVE #3: *In the process of responding to challenges by Jewish opponents, emerging Christianity adjusted or added to Jesus-traditions teachings and nuances not authentic to Jesus' ministry*

[Accordingly, teachings ascribed to Jesus—and impinging on Jews & Judaism—should not be viewed only as an undifferentiated mass.]

EARLY CHRISTIAN BELIEF & PRACTICE	CHALLENGES POSED BY JEWISH RESISTANCE	RESULTANT ADJUSTMENTS OF OR ADDITIONS TO JESUS TRADITIONS
Example I— Gentile-Christians ignore Jewish dietary laws	Jewish Challenge: How can you Christians profess to fulfill God's covenant while violating the laws of kashrut?	Christian Response: ". . . Do you not see that whatever goes into a man from outside cannot defile him. . . ?" (Thus he declared all foods clean.") [Mk. 7:18–19]
Example II— Christians argue the legitimacy of Jesus' messianic credentials	Jewish Challenge: Elijah, the herald authenticating the true Messiah, has not yet come. [Mk. 9:11— ". . . Why do the scribes say that first Elijah must come?"]	Christian Response: [Mk. 9:13—". . . I tell you that Elijah has come. . . ."] → [Mt. 17:13—"Then the disciples understood that he was speaking to them of John the Baptist"] [+ Antipas (=Ahab)/ Herodias (=Jezebel) imagery, etc.]
Example III— Christians claim Jesus was resurrected	Jewish Challenge #1: Jesus was not resurrected.	Christian Response: The fashioning of the empty tomb narrative.
	Jewish Challenge #2: Tomb empty because disciples stole the body.	Christian Response: Theft story a fiction: [Mt. 27:15b "And this story has been spread among the Jews to this day"].

PERSPECTIVE #4: *Study of Mark, Matthew and Luke in parallel columns suggests that later writers intensified the anti-Judaism of their sources.*

[Anti-Judaism may decrease as we regress toward Christian origins.]

PERSPECTIVE #5: *The reason why passages in the Jewish Bible seem to predict the coming of Jesus is that Christian tradition came to model Jesus' image to conform to it with Jewish revered* with the Jesus who himself decries the Pharisees with the words: "You serpents, you brood of vipers, how are you to escape being sentenced to hell?" (Mt 23:33); or the Jesus who, on the one hand, says, "Love your enemies . . . , pray for those who persecute you" (Mt 5:44), with the Jesus who says (to "Jews who . . . believed in him" [Jn 8:31]!) "you are of your father the devil . . . , a murderer from the beginning . . . , a liar and the father of lies . . ." (8:44f.)?

How is the Jesus who is fully within and an exemplar of fidelity to Judaism, citing and reciting the Shema, the Golden Rule, and God's coming kingdom as preeminent teachings, to be reconciled with gospel traditions wherein Jesus claims to be greater than the sabbath (Mk 2:28) and greater than the Temple (Mt 12:6), and insists that his own teachings actually supersede the law of Moses by repeating the refrain: "You have heard that it was said to the men of old . . . , but I say unto you" (Mt 5:21–28)?

Should not our laities be helped to view these conflicting images of Jesus *developmentally?* This is *Perspective #1:* that *changes in Christianity's developing self-perception vis-à-vis Judaism occasioned corresponding adjustments in portrayals of Jesus' stance toward Jews and Judaism.*

This means, for example, that during Christianity's pre-Pauline phase, when emergent Christianity perceived itself *within* Judaism, this self-perception naturally occasioned the preserving or generating of traditions portraying Jesus as an exemplar of *fidelity* toward Judaism. But later, preeminently under the influence of Pauline thought, Christianity became more conscious of its own individuality and *regretful* that so many Jews continued to abstain from entering the church (cf. especially Rom 9–11); then it was that the figure of Jesus came, in a natural kind of way, to be adjusted by developing Christian tradition so as to reflect that regret at what was construed as Jewish blindness or opaqueness to the truths of Christianity. Subsequently, when interchanges between Christian missionaries and Jewish opponents, particularly the Pharisees, became increasingly hostile, Christianity's regret was now supplanted by an intensifying *hostility* toward Jews,[3] with the figure of Jesus becoming enlisted in support of this accrued bitterness, Jesus himself now becoming portrayed as hostile toward Jews and their Pharisaic teachers.[4]

Some may deem this "working hypothesis" unworkable. Yet it may prove instructive despite its inadequacies. At least five vulnerabilities occur to me: (1) Nothing absolutely precludes Jesus himself from having espoused *all three* positions: i.e., fidelity, regret, and hostility. (2) Since scholarship has achieved no consensus in distinguishing gospel statements authentic to Jesus from those issuing instead from the later church, the attempt to compartmentalize various Jesus images does seem problematic . . . and arbitrary. (3) It might be charged that Jewish readers tend to gravitate, even if involuntarily (and, in some cases, unknowingly), toward the methods of liberal form criticism—applying these methods in a fashion that conveniently reinforces the *Jewish* view of Jesus. Starkly put, the more one can strip away gospel traditions attributable to the later (especially *Gentile*) church, the more characteristically *Jewish* the Jesus-who-remains will turn out to be—especially since traditions most easily assignable to the later church may naturally include those which most vigorously qualify Jesus' fidelity to Judaism and/or his fellow people. Some will therefore decry this Jewish approach as circular. (4) In practice, recourse to rabbinic literature in order to discover presumed parallels to Jesus' teachings (a major avenue by which to establish Jesus' proximity to Pharisaism and fidelity to Judaism) has often been methodologically flawed.[5] (5) It becomes arduous to explain why early Christianity traced its origins to a Jesus who was presumably in no significant way different from the diversified Judaism(s) of his own day.

In response, however, at least some scholars would argue that the insuperable problems we encounter in validating this approach still fail to invalidate it entirely. Part of Perspective #1 (i.e., the *upper* row of the arrow-diagram) may remain persuasive to some: that, generally speaking, in the course of the first century, Christianity's developing self-perception vis-à-vis Jews/Judaism most probably did express itself in consecutive phases of *consonance,* then *regret,* and then supplemented or ultimately supplanted by *hostility.* At least some corresponding adjustments in Jesus' image, reflective of these changes, would inevitably have been forthcoming—would it not be unrealistic to argue otherwise?

Problems encountered in analyzing particular gospel passages do not necessarily impugn the validity of the hypothesis *in general,* since, paradoxically, what breaks down is not so much the hypothesis as the attempts to prove it! That Jesus' immediate followers remained within the synagogue and continued to abide by Jewish practice argues that they must have identified the historical Jesus himself as having been at least in general consonance with Jewish belief and practice; meanwhile, the intensity of gospel denunciations of Jews can still most plausibly be assigned to the period well after Jesus' death, when Christianity's attitude toward many Jews had become suffused with hostility.

The case for Perspective #1 may also be reinforced by its possible compatibility with Perspectives #2–5, and decisions as to their plausibility. While there is some unavoidable circularity to such reasoning, a temporary suspension of judgment is probably a permissible request. At the very least, however, *awareness* of this Jewish perspective is indispensable for participants in dialogue, irrespective of conclusions concerning its validity.

It is precisely this awareness that has often been benignly withheld from our laities, to the tremendous detriment of Jewish-Christian relations! For since most *Jewish* laypersons have never heard that Jesus' denigrations of the Jews may be instead denunciations by the later church expressed through his gospel image, they naturally identify Jesus himself as the exponent of such anti-Judaism. No wonder they end up taking a Jesus possibly faithful to Judaism and then turn him into an apostate who deprecated the essentials of his own religion!

Nor are the Jewish laity any more misled here than were the rabbis of the Talmud who viewed gospel traditions in the same uncritical fashion. Not distinguishing between what Jesus may have said and what the later church said he said, the Talmud likewise concluded that Jesus was an apostate.[6] Given the primitive state of gospel study in the early rabbinic age, however, the miscomprehensions of the rabbis are understandable. But how rationalize the reality that most Jewish laypersons today, one and one-half millennia later, still echo these same misconceptions? Is this forward progress? No, this is *lateral* pacing!

On the other hand, what incentive is there to implement changes in the Jewish arena without assurance of corresponding progress in the *Christian* lay sector, wherein most Christians continue to ascribe gospel indictments of Jews and Judaism to Jesus personally, with their assessment of Judaism today thereby unavoidably influenced accordingly? And, in this connection, I feel it is self-deluding even to attempt combating negative stereotyping of Jews and Judaism, prevalent among the Christian laity, unless, as part of this resolve, we also enlighten them concerning the dynamics of how these stereotypes first arose—including the dynamics of how the gospels themselves evolved. To bypass such a process is tantamount to treating only the symptoms while ignoring the cause.

By such a refusal, we would render an injustice to the integrity of the religious quest for truth by sanctioning what I consider a "cafeteria approach" to gospel traditions: allowing Jewish and Christian laypersons freely to select whatever they wish, while we withhold from them *informed* opinions concerning the relative merits of what is being displayed! Thus, the average Jew selects a depiction of Jesus as an apostate from his people even as most Christians accept a Jesus-image who seems to caricature both Jews and Judaism. Here we may be reminded of a woman whose son had served in the army during World War II. Asked where he had been stationed, she replied, "Oh, in the Illusions!" While she meant the "Aleutians," the mistake is instructive. For we have indeed consigned our laities to the "Illusions"!

PERSPECTIVE #2

In our efforts to extricate ourselves from this dilemma, a *second* fundamental perspective requires our considered attention. It constitutes a spin-off from the first and asserts that *the various ways in which Paul's theology was understood influenced the evolution of the gospel portraits of Jesus.*

Paul's epistles are our earliest Christian writings and Paul's thinking may have been vitally determinative of the directions taken by differing segments of early Christianity, both by those adhering to Pauline views (whether or not they interpreted Paul correctly) and by those resistant to Paul but forced nevertheless to come to grips with his thinking (whether or not they interpreted that thinking correctly). Throughout this discussion, my emphasis will not be so much on what Paul actually said or intended, but rather on the influential role those who *interpreted* Paul (even in widely diverging fashions) may have played in the way in which Jesus came to be portrayed in later gospel traditions.

As the diagram indicates, the conceptualization here would be that the earliest images of the historical Jesus and his teachings in many a case passed through the filter of Paul's interpretation concerning the meaning of the Christ (and thus as well through the filter of others' interpretations of Paul's interpretation), the consequence of this filtering process being that Jesus' image and teachings were not simply preserved but also embellished and in some cases significantly transformed. With respect to subsequent Jewish-Christian relations, at least three themes of decisive importance may be envisioned as having been generated through this process, each bearing the impress either of what Paul himself preached, or how others construed or misconstrued that preaching: (1) The motif of rejection of the Law of Moses (construed or *mis*construed on the basis of, e.g., Galatians 2:16; 3:10–11,23–26; Romans 7:1–6); (2) The motif of Christian missionaries turning the focus of their preaching away from Jews and toward Gentiles instead (construed or *mis*construed on the basis of, e.g.,

Galatians 1:15f.; 2:7; 3:14); (3) the motif of Jews being superseded by Gentiles as God's chosen people (construed or *mis*construed on the basis of, e.g., Galatians 4:22–30; Romans 9:6–13,25–26,30–32, qualified by 11:23–29).

Much of Jewish scholarship, however, and a significant segment of scholarship in general, has indeed denied that Jesus ever actually "broke" with the law of Moses, denied that Jesus ever counseled a turning from the Jews to the Gentiles instead, and denied that he ever sanctioned the notion of the Jews being superseded by Gentiles. Since these three themes have contributed centrally to the stereotyping of Jesus, by *some* Jews, as an apostate, as well as to the supersessionist and triumphalist theology of *some* Christians past and present, the suggestion that these motifs derive more from how Paul was interpreted or misinterpreted than from what Jesus personally said or did is sobering— but it can only be sobering to those who are genuinely aware of the possibility!

On the issue of Jesus' attitude toward the law, for example, those so aware are sensitive to the following problems:

1. Why did Paul experience such violent opposition from the pillars of the Jerusalem church (James, Cephas, and John) when he ate with Gentiles (and presumably broke Jewish dietary laws), and began bringing Gentiles directly into the Christian fold (cf. Gal 1:18–2:21)? After all, were not these actions apparently consistent with Jesus' own instructions (if, as some gospel texts suggest, Jesus himself had indeed departed from the Law [e.g., Mk 7:1–6,8–9,13–15, and especially 18b–19; also 2:18–20,23–28; 3:1–5] and himself had counseled or predicted a turning to Gentiles [e.g., Mt 21:43; 22:8–10; the implication of Lk 4:24–27; 14:24; cf. Mt 8:10–12])? Why did not James, Cephas, and John recognize Paul's *consonance with Jesus*—why did they not themselves remember Jesus' own stance (James being Jesus' own brother, Cephas his foremost disciple, and John likewise one of the twelve)?

2. If Jesus had indeed "declared all foods clean" (Mk 7:19), why did Peter need to receive a thrice-stated revelation (Acts 10:9–17) concerning what he should have clearly remembered from Jesus personally, with even this special revelation leaving him "inwardly perplexed as to what . . . [this] might mean"?

3. If Jesus had publicly transgressed the sabbath or publicly justified such transgression by his disciples (e.g., Mk 2:23–3:5), how could Paul's Judaizing opponents in Galatia have, in so flagrant a way, insisted on Jewish calendrical observance (Gal 4:9–11)—or, more widely, on general adherence to the same law which Jesus had presumably disavowed?

4. Why, when Paul argued the issue of the law, did he not draw for support upon Jesus' specific *teachings* (i.e., teachings along the lines of those later recorded in the *gospels*), instead of arguing *only* on the general ground that faith in Christ, rather than the keeping of the Torah, constitutes the basis for attaining salvation? Surely such recourse to specific teachings of Jesus (similar to those discoverable by us later in the gospels) would have been not only useful but (given the authority associated with Jesus) vitally persuasive—especially since food and sabbath issues were sorely troubling problems for Paul (Gal 2:11–14; Rom 14:1–4,13–23; Gal 4:10; Rom 14:5–6).

All such examples underpin the argument that it was only *subsequent* to Paul's break with the law that Jesus-traditions, whether potentially supportive[7] of Paul's attitude or reactive against it,[8] were fashioned in direct response to issues raised for the first time only years after Jesus' death.

My own reservations about Perspective #2 include four in particular: (1) Does it exaggerate Paul's influence? Departures from the law in emerging churches do not seem to have been single-handedly engineered by Paul;[9] moreover, Gentile membership in some churches (e.g., Rome, Antioch) is not traceable exclusively, if at all, to Paul. (2) It is problematic to "saddle" Paul with every significant Christian departure from Judaism, as if Paul were the founder of a Christianity manifesting no threads of connectedness with Jesus. (3) The possible relevance of Jesus' eschatological expectations for the near future is left unaddressed. For example, since the prophets themselves make allowance for possible inclusion of Gentiles in the "end of days" (Isa 2:2f.; 49:6; 51:4; 56:8; cf. 45:22; 66:19; Micah 4:1ff.; Zech 2:11; cf. 8:20–23), Paul's own turning to Gentiles is arguably an extrapolation of what had been *latent* within a Jesus who not only expected the imminent end of the world order, but did so within the parameters of Jewish scriptural anticipation of *Gentile* involvement in that new era! (4) Still further, some critics may argue that examples of *consonance* between Paul and later gospel traditions, as emphasized by Perspective #2, are easily explained as a function of different writers naturally preserving a commonality of tradition or expressing a commonality of viewpoint—rather than necessarily a function of the evangelists' explicit dependence on interpretations or misinterpretations of Paul himself.

Nonetheless, that Paul actually produced writings, that they possibly were the *only* pre-70 Christian writings produced and remaining extant, and that they were provocative and deemed significant enough to achieve canonization (or to require it as a means of controlling how they would be interpreted[10]), are all factors possibly restoring to Paul whatever eminence he loses by challenges that there must have been other missionaries to Gentiles besides him. Moreover, even as we acknowledge connecting threads from Jesus to emergent Christianity, Paul's demonstrated capacity for *reinterpreting* Jesus' significance along lines probably substantially divergent from earliest understandings (witness his elaboration of the themes of "crucifixion" and "resurrection") permits the insistence that, with Paul, Christianity experienced renewal, redirection, indeed radical transformation.

If, e.g., Galatians 2:15f. requires that Jews, to be saved, must actually *forgo* the law, this would be no mere latency from Jesus! When Paul *reverses* the sequence for salvation, such that now "the full number of Gentiles" will actually *precede* disbelieving Israel (Rom 11:25–26), this would be more than developing a latency within Jesus! Respecting supersession, when Paul argues that the covenant has skipped from Abraham to Christ, with membership now restricted to those in Christ irrespective of whether they are Israel by descent (Rom 9:6ff.), this exceeds a latency from Jesus!

And how best resolve the four anomalies listed above if not through Perspective #2: that certain themes in the gospel portraits of Jesus, cohering with Pauline theology, though apparently unknown and unappealed to before or during Paul's day, are most likely the result of Pauline influence on the formation of the gospels' images of Jesus? It was Pauline thought, years after Jesus' ministry, which first stimulated the raising of these issues of the law, the turning to the Gentiles, and Gentiles' supersession of the Jews, and advocates of these themes who then began to press them in earnest. In terms of Paul himself, Jesus' intimate followers had vigorously opposed Paul because they had perceived him as distancing himself from what they clearly remembered as having been Jesus' own fidelity to the law and to the Jewish people.

That the influence of Paul's thinking could have stimulated the gospel writers into constructing images of Jesus so at variance from the original personage is an idea which, while long debated by scholars,[11] has never even been heard of by most laypersons, whether Christian or Jewish. This is largely because they have not been made sufficiently aware even that Paul's epistles *preceded* the completed gospels! Most laypersons assume, since Paul's epistles are later than Jesus' ministry, and the gospels describe that ministry, that Paul, therefore, must be later than the gospels—a conclusion which, while logical, is also wrong.

By analogy, many paintings have been discovered to be only super-impositions over earlier works, such that, when the superimposed embel-lishment is removed, the newly-revealed original is strikingly different from what we had observed before. Similarly, removal of post-Pauline embellishments would no doubt reveal an earlier portrait of Jesus quite at variance from the later depictions. By our depriving our laities of this realization, we are preventing *Jews* from recognizing the possible fidelity of Jesus to Judaism, and *Christians* from realizing Jesus' possible appre-ciation both of the law and of Judaism's vitality and ongoing covenantal relationship to God!

PERSPECTIVE #3

Not only are our laities generally unaware of the time-lag between the ministry of Jesus and the production of completed gospels, but they are likewise unaware of the plethora of problems arising for emerging churches during this interval. Despite the gospels' ostensible preoccupa-tion with retelling the details of Jesus' ministry back around the year 30 C.E., in reality the gospels were also addressing these more recently surfacing issues. So formidable were some of these problems that Chris-tianity inevitably had to enlist the authoritative image of Jesus himself for assistance in solving them—even though these were problems arising only well after his ministry, and concerning which he had neither involve-ment nor antecedent awareness. That is to say, the gospel writers con-ceived that their own immediate problems had already originated in the time of Jesus, years earlier, and that the answers to their problems were therefore discoverable in his words and deeds. So disposed, they often had to recast his actual teachings in order to render them germane for later circumstances which, in reality, these teachings had not originally been intended to address.

Of particular interest to this discussion are challenges posed by Jews to the validity of Jesus' messianic credentials and to the validity of the Christian preachment, suggestive in turn of *Perspective #3: that in the*

process of responding to challenges by Jewish opponents, emerging Chris-
tianity adjusted or added to Jesus-traditions teachings and nuances not
authentic to Jesus' ministry; accordingly, teachings ascribed to Jesus—and
impinging on Jews and Judaism—should not be viewed only as an undif-
ferentiated mass.

Thus, in the case of Example I on the diagram, when some of the
Christian community began to ignore Jewish dietary laws, Jewish opponents inevitably posed a challenge: how can Christians profess to fulfill
God's covenant while violating the laws of *kashrut?* In responding to
this problem, Mark enlisted the aid of the Jesus-figure, but to do so
had to adjust a teaching of Jesus to mean something somewhat other
than what Jesus personally had intended. Mark redirected Jesus' words,
"Do you not see that whatever goes into a man from outside cannot
defile him?" (7:18) to mean (in 7:19b) that ". . . (Thus he declared all
foods clean.)" This parenthetical comment derives from Mark, not
Jesus.[12] While Jesus' intent may have been to teach that what truly
matters most is one's internal moral and spiritual consciousness, Mark
applied Jesus' words to the different problem of Jewish dietary laws, so
as to address a recent challenge arising for the first time only after
Jesus' ministry, i.e., in the interval between 30 C.E. and the composition of Mark around 70 C.E.

Similarly, in Example II, Jews challenged the legitimacy of Jesus'
messianic credentials by arguing that Elijah, the herald anticipating and
authenticating the true Messiah, had yet to appear. Ultimately, Christian tradition took the figure of John the Baptist and conformed *him* to
Elijah's image.[13] Additionally, it attributed John's death to a conspiracy
by a wicked king and queen, Herod Antipas and Herodias, thereby
conforming their role as well to Ahab and Jezebel, who had sought
Elijah's life. The artificiality of this solution is evinced by our recourse
to Josephus, who correctly describes John the Baptist with none of these
Elijah trappings, and conveys a far more credible account of how, why,
and where he died.[14]

As a third example, Jews challenged traditions of Jesus' resurrection. Christians, attempting to refute that challenge, came to believe in
an empty tomb tradition (unmentioned and, one might submit, unknown by Paul). When Jews, in turn, countered by attributing the alleged emptiness of the tomb to the disciples' theft of the body, Matthew
had to go to great lengths to refute their allegation (27:62–66; 28:11–
15). Since the Jewish suggestion of a theft was an inevitable response to
the empty tomb story, the fact that *Mark* had failed to address it implies

that the empty tomb tradition first surfaced either with Mark himself or only shortly before him—it is a Christian response to a Jewish challenge arising between Jesus' ministry in 30 C.E. and the completion of Mark around 70 C.E.

Though these examples are illustrative of matters which have been analyzed by scholars and clergy for decades now, our laities are yet, for the most part, shielded from this entire discussion. Accordingly, they are prevented from recognizing that many of the teachings ascribed to Jesus and impinging on Jews and Judaism do not originate with Jesus. Rather, they reflect concerns of the later church in responding to Jewish challenges arising only subsequent to Jesus' ministry.

PERSPECTIVE #4

Study of the Gospels of Mark, Matthew, and Luke in parallel columns reveals that later writers intensified the anti-Judaism of their sources such that one can plausibly argue that anti-Judaism may decrease as we regress toward Christian origins. Most laypersons, whether Christian or Jewish, are unfamiliar with this *fourth* perspective because they are unaware that a procedure for comparing the first three gospels in parallel columns is standard scholarly practice and has led most scholars to conclude that both Matthew and Luke have not only frequently copied Mark but have also frequently *altered* him. It would thus emerge as plausible that anti-Jewish nuances present in Matthew and Luke, yet absent from the parallel material in Mark, could be a function of the later editors' own inclinations, conditioned perhaps by the tense climate of Christian-Jewish discourse in their day. The shielding of the laity from studying these gospels in parallel columns has been detrimental to Jewish-Christian relations because it has prevented laypersons from discerning how systematically a later writer, e.g., Matthew, has heightened the anti-Judaism of one of his sources, such as Mark.

Thus, for example, while in Mark the Jewish officials, thinking Jesus guilty, seek *true* testimony against him (14:55), Matthew puts it that they knew he was innocent and therefore had to seek *false* testimony *ab initio* (26:59).[15] Matthew adds to Mark the infamous "Blood Curse" wherein the Jews are alleged to have volunteered: "Let his blood be on us and on our children!" (27:25). Whereas, in Mark, Jesus and a Jewish "scribe" exchange camaraderie (12:28–34a), Matthew edits out the friendship and turns the exchange into confrontation (22:34–40). Parables of Jesus originally exhibiting no animosity toward Jews or Judaism have definitely been anti-Jewishly allegorized by Matthew and Luke and, to a lesser degree, by Mark as well.[16]

Indeed, it can be plausibly argued that what Matthew and Luke did in editing Mark was likewise accomplished by Mark in editing traditions antecedent to his own writing. Teachings of Jesus, not originally uttered in the context of controversy, have definitely been transformed by Mark himself into confrontations.[17] How salutary for the cause of Jewish-Christian relations would be the realization by our laities that, the further we recede into earliest Christianity—approaching the time frame of the historical Jesus—the more evident it becomes that intense expressions of anti-Judaism in the gospels are a function, not of Jesus' ministry, but rather of the later church.

PERSPECTIVE #5

Nor should a *fifth* perspective receive any less emphasis: *One of the reasons why passages in the Jewish Bible seem to predict the coming of Jesus is that Christian tradition came to model Jesus' image in conformity with Jewish scriptural imagery.* This fundamental concept is almost entirely unheard of among our laities.

For centuries, Jews have been bombarded by missionaries and now also by slick pamphleteers and media preachers drumming home a steady staccato of so-called "prooftexts" from Jewish scripture so as to demonstrate how Jesus fulfilled biblical predictions of the coming of the Messiah. To many scholars and clergy, the seemingly uncanny correspondence between these passages and details of Jesus' ministry is hardly uncanny at all—for developing gospel traditions consciously fashioned details of Jesus' life so as precisely to match the so-called predictions.[18]

But to the uninformed Jewish layperson, these pamphleteers and preachers are befuddling when they trumpet the apparent correspondence of the gospels' Jesus with Isaiah's "Suffering Servant" (42:1–4; 49:1–6; 50:4–9; 52:13–53:12); or of Jesus' entry to Jerusalem on a donkey with its presumed prediction by the Hebrew prophet, Zechariah (9:9); or of the scene and words of Jesus on the cross with imagery from Psalms (e.g., 22:1,6–8,16–18; 69:21); or of an apparent solar eclipse during Jesus' crucifixion (Lk 23:44–45) with its seeming anticipation by the Hebrew prophets Amos (8:9) and Joel (2:31). To many Christian laypersons, these scripture-pounding preachers seem so persuasive that one must wonder at the obtuseness of Jews who seem incapable of recognizing as intuitively obvious scripture's specific anticipation of Jesus as the Christ.[19] Jews, meanwhile, though not knowing how to explain these phenomena, nonetheless do know that this onslaught of prooftexts elicits their ill-will toward Christians whom they view as encroaching on Jewish sensibilities.

This dilemma originated with Paul, who insisted that Jesus died *in accordance with scripture* and rose *in accordance with scripture*. He therefore rendered it inevitable by this line of argument that other Christians would likewise look to Jewish scripture—at the time, their *only* scripture—in an attempt to "prove" their arguments.

It is vital to recognize that the gospel authors did not possess data sufficient to flesh out their accounts of Jesus' ministry. After all, some or all of them lived outside Palestine, and they were writing forty to seventy years after Jesus' death. Much that once had been known about Jesus by some had by now become forgotten. Moreover, precisely because the Second Coming had been expected so imminently, preserving details of the ministry had never been a priority concern. Rather, for early Christian theology, it was the significance of the crucifixion and belief in the resurrection which were preeminent, not the details of Jesus' ministry (to which Paul, for example, but rarely seems to allude).

Not surprisingly, the completed production of the gospels coincided with the time frame of the dying off of many of the eyewitnesses of Jesus' ministry.[20] For it was the loss of witnesses which now rendered imperative the reduction of oral recall to written form. At the same time, however, the fading of eyewitnesses from the scene made that recall all the more difficult. Yet the Jewish Bible could prove of potential assistance! Believing not only that Jesus was the Christ, but also that Jewish scripture had predicted the Christ, the early Christians inevitably deduced that Jewish scripture had been predicting Jesus in particular, and that Jewish scripture was therefore essentially construable as a book about "Christ Jesus." If, then, no sufficient details were still available or remembered about Jesus' ministry, Jewish scripture could itself be combed as a ready repository of missing clues to which the image of Jesus could then be confidently conformed because it was assumed that, in point of fact, Jesus' ministry and Jewish scripture were indeed fully congruent one to the other.

Thus, the uncanny similarity of the Jesus-image to Isaiah's "Suffering Servant" is the result of the gospels' specific modeling or conforming of Jesus to the "Suffering Servant" image. Some details of the scene of Jesus on the cross[21] "fulfill" Psalm 22 because they were *taken* from Psalm 22! The idea for the solar eclipse during the crucifixion in Luke is derived from, and conformed to, the solar vocabulary of Amos and Joel (even though a solar eclipse during *Passover's full moon* would have been astronomically impossible). Matthew, misunderstanding Zechariah's prediction, erroneously had Jesus ride into Jerusalem on *two* animals simultaneously—a telltale indication of the lengths to which gospel traditions would go in accommodating the Jesus-image to Jewish scripture.

This dynamic recalls for us the story of a farmer who once arrayed his barn wall with thirteen bull's-eyes, with an arrow imbedded in the center of each. Appearances differed from reality, however, because he had shot the arrows *first* and only *afterwards* had he painted a bull's-eye around each one! The so-called "predictions" from Jewish scripture are like the arrows, with Jesus' image in the gospel traditions being the bull's-eye consciously (though in full faith and confidence) painted around the arrow.

Were this realization, long accepted by many scholars,[22] to be shared with the *Jewish* laity, it would immediately dissipate their befuddlement with missionaries who themselves are ignorant of this dynamic. And were it shared with the *Christian* laity, it might alter their widespread assessment of Jews as peculiarly ignorant of obvious truth, and likewise serve as a deterrent to a mentality pejoratively defined as "bibliolatry," i.e., worship of the Bible in lieu of God. Bibliolatry in this country has become a subtle form of idolatry, distortive of and subversive of the goals of enlightened religion. I submit that, insofar as scholars and clergy refrain from imparting such insights to their laity, they are failing to honor a fundamental commitment of scholarship—to discover or uncover and deliver truth!

In summation, I have proposed that foremost on our agenda over the next twenty years should be the translation of the results of New Testament scholarship into the *lay* arena—so that "facts" will be preferred over "fancies," "history" over "histrionics," "science" over "superstition."[23] The search for truth entails examination and not just unquestioning acceptance of the Bible, and while such examination may be "traumatic to the uninformed public, . . . the trauma is no greater than" that which scholars, clergy, and tens of thousands of university students have passed through in their religious studies courses—all of whom have survived, and many of whom have deeply appreciated the insights they have gained, and have become better church and synagogue members by virtue of that knowledge.[24]

I am reminded of a conference of scholars held a number of years ago, involving my Quaker alma mater, Haverford College. Prominent theologians were exchanging views concerning the essence of Jesus' teachings. A venerable, elderly laywoman, seated in the rear of the audience, was fascinated by what she was hearing now for the very first time in her life—ideas about the Bible that she felt had been kept from her for her seventy-five years! Impatient at the way she and the other laypersons were being excluded from involvement and participation in the discussion, she rose, with Bible in hand, and unceremoniously interrupted the deliberations.

"I am asserting," she began, "my prerogative to speak when and as moved by the Spirit. I read here in my Bible," she continued, "that Jesus said, 'Feed my lambs' (Jn 21:15). He never said, 'Feed my giraffes.' Brothers, why not put the food where the *lambs* can get it?!"

NOTES

1. *The Chaplain,* Vol. 2, #12 (December, 1945), p. 42.

2. The selection, distillation, and manner of formulating these five Jewish perspectives are my own, along with the diagrammatic representations. Not all perspectives are expressly espoused by every Jewish scholar, but the compatibility or coherence of the perspectives vis-à-vis each other justify the claim that they typify Jewish scholarship broadly construed. Readers are directed not only to individual Jewish authors but, more productively, to helpful surveys of Jewish scholarship on Jesus and Christian origins, including the following (listed alphabetically): Sh. Ben Chorin, *Jesus im Judentum* (Wuppertal, 1970); idem, "The Image of Jesus in Modern Judaism," *Journal of Ecumenical Studies* 11 (1974): 401–430; H. Danby, *The Jew and Christianity: Some Phases . . . of the Jewish Attitude* (London, 1927); D. Hagner, *The Jewish Reclamation of Jesus* (Grand Rapids, 1984); W. Jacob, *Christianity through Jewish Eyes* (Cincinnati, 1974); J. Jocz, *The Jewish People and Jesus Christ,* repr. (Grand Rapids, 1979); G. Lindeskog, *Die Jesusfrage im Neuzeitlichen Judentum,* repr. (Darmstadt, 1973); C. G. Montefiore, "Jewish Conceptions of Christianity," *Hibbert Journal* 28 (1929–1930): 246–260; S. Sandmel, *We Jews and Jesus,* repr. (New York, 1973); T. Walker, *Jewish Views of Jesus* (New York, 1931).

3. While some scholars argue that Christianity's ranks by the end of the first century were already predominantly *Gentile,* others insist on a continued high proportion of *Jewish*-Christians. On the basis of the latter view, hostility (in this case toward *non-Christian Jews* yet still perceived as *fellow*-Jews) would also here still be assignable to the post-70 time frame, and "Jesus' " stance of hostility would also here be a function of changes in (*Jewish-*)Christians' self-perception vis-à-vis, in this case, their non-Christian but still *fellow* Jews.

4. Many Jewish scholars might subsume within the *first phase* these intimations of *consonance:* the Great Commandment (Mk 12:28–34; cf. *Berakhoth* 61b; *Shabbat* 31a); the Lord's Prayer (Mt 6:9–13); the theme of the coming of God's kingdom; and, prior to their allegorical expansion, many of Jesus' parables (i.e., in varying ways Jewish scholars have compared Matthew 20:1–16 with *Jer. Ber.* ii.3c, *Eccles. R.* 5:11, *S. of Songs R.* 6:2, and *Deut R.* 6:1; Mt 22:1–14 and Lk 14:16–24 with *Shabbat* 153a, *Jer. Sanh.* vi.23c, and *Lamentations R.* 4:2; Lk 15:11–32 with *Deut. R.* 2:24, *Sot.* 9:15 and *Sanh.* 38b; Lk 15:8–10 and Mt 13:44–46 with *Eccles. R.* 9:7 and *S. of Songs R.* 1:1,9). Reflecting the *second phase*—manifestations of *regret*—would be preeminently Romans 9–11 (particularly 9:1ff.; 10:1ff.; 11:1,11f.,25–26). The *third period* would be seen as manifesting *hostility* through *words attributed to Jesus* (e.g., "woes" against the Pharisees [Mt 23] and passages in John which seem either to be abrasive toward Jews [e.g., 5:42,45–46; 6:53; 8:23f.,37–38,44–47] or to present Jesus as outside the fold of the Jewish people [e.g., Jn 10:34; 13:33])—and through channels *other than Jesus' words* (e.g., the formulation of the Sanhedrin trial [Mk 14:53ff. and par.] and the Barabbas episode [Mk 15:6ff. and par.] with its infamous "blood curse" [Mt 27:24–25], in addition to frequent editorial characterizations of Jews and their leaders, impugning their motives and maligning their conduct).

5. See M. J. Cook, "Jesus and the Pharisees: the Problem as It Stands Today," *Journal of Ecumenical Studies* 15 [1978], pp. 441–460.

6. Major treatments of rabbinic passages construed as referring to Jesus include: R. T. Herford, *Christianity in Talmud and Midrash* (London, 1903); J. Klausner, *Jesus of Nazareth,* trans. H. Danby, repr. (New York, 1943), pp. 17–54; M. Goldstein, *Jesus in the Jewish Tradition* (New York, 1950); J. Z. Lauterbach, "Jesus in the Talmud," *Rabbinic Essays* (Cincinnati, 1951), pp. 471–570. See also D. R. Catchpole, *The Trial of Jesus: A Study in the Gospels and Jewish Historiography from 1770 to the Present Day* (Leiden, 1971), pp. 1–71.

7. Thus, e.g., Mark, writing forty years after Jesus' death and a number of years after Paul as well, described Jesus through the filter of Paul's view of the law and Paul's disparagement of legalism per se—as Mark understood them. There accordingly emerges out of Mark's gospel an image of Jesus who breaks with the law, as is evidenced particularly in traditions of Jesus' controversies with the Pharisees (cf. my volume, *Mark's Treatment of the Jewish Leaders* [Leiden, 1978]).

8. Matthew, taking issue with Paul's denigration of law, altered Mark's portrayal by constructing a Jesus intent on preserving and even more fully observing every "jot and tittle" of the law, while also warning that he who "relaxes . . . the least of these commandments and [likewise] teaches men [to do] so, shall be called least in the kingdom of heaven" (Mt 5:17ff.). In reality, this was not actually Jesus speaking, but rather Matthew attacking Paul for relaxing the commandments and teaching others to do likewise; this was Matthew presenting a Jesus so legalistic that he advances a new law which supersedes and renders

passé earlier commitments to legalism (cf. my essay, "Interpreting 'Pro-Jewish' Passages in Matthew," *Hebrew Union College Annual* 54 [1983], pp. 135–146).

9. Cf. Galatians 2:11f., where the practice of eating with Gentiles is not expressly said to have originated at Paul's behest; and where Cephas (possibly on his own initiative) also ate with them until the arrival of James' emissaries occasioned a crisis.

10. Cf. M. S. Enslin, "Once Again, Luke and Paul," *Zeitschrift für die Neutestamentliche Wissenschaft* 61 (1970): 253–71.

11. In response to those who will insist that there is no compelling evidence that the gospel writers were acquainted with Paul's epistles, note how Paul himself attests that others knew of them. He quotes his opponents (2 Cor 10:10) to the effect that "his letters are weighty and strong . . ."! On the problem, cf. Enslin, art. cit.; also, idem, " 'Luke' and Paul," *Journal of the American Oriental Society* 58 (1938): 81ff. J. Knox puts the matter as follows: "I agree with Enslin that it is all but incredible that such a man as Luke . . . should have been 'totally unaware that this hero of his had ever written letters. . . . Too many important churches owed their existence to [Paul] for his name not to have been held in reverence in many areas and his work remembered. . . .' Luke knew, or at least knew of, letters of Paul . . ." ("Acts and the Pauline Letter Corpus," *Studies in Luke Acts,* L. E. Keck and J. L. Martyn, ed. [Philadelphia: Fortress, 1980], pp. 279–87, esp. p. 283).

12. It is perhaps instructive that, in the parallel episode in Matthew 15:15f., the parenthetical statement is absent (omitted?).

13. While this solution is only implicit in Mark 9:13: ". . . I tell you that Elijah has [already] come . . . ," it is rendered explicit by the parallel passage, Matthew 17:13: "Then the disciples understood that he was speaking to them of John the Baptist."

14. *Antiquities* XVIII:116–119 (Whiston edition: XVIII.v.2).

15. Viewing this positively, one could say that Matthew's adjustment tends to accentuate Jesus' innocence even more than ever, where innocence equals righteousness. Yet Matthew accomplishes this by impugning the Jews' motives and behavior.

16. E.g., Mark 12:1–12; Matthew 21:33–43; 22:1–10; Luke 14:16–24; 20:9–19.

17. Cook, *Mark's Treatment,* pp. 57–76.

18. Cf. B. Lindars, *New Testament Apologetic: the Doctrinal Significance of the Old Testament Quotations* (London, 1961); J. Daniélou, *From Shadows to Reality: Studies in the Biblical Typology of the Fathers* (London, 1960); G. W. H. Lampe, "The Reasonableness of Typology," and K. J. Woollcombe, "The Biblical Origins and Patristic Development of Typology," in *Essays on Typology* (Naperville, Ill., 1957), pp. 9–75; R. H. Smith, "Exodus Typology in the Fourth Gospel," *Journal of Biblical Literature* 81 (1962), pp. 329–342; N. M. Cohen, *Jewish Bible Personages in the New Testament* (Lanham, Md.: University Press of America, 1989).

19. Laypersons so disposed may readily subscribe to Paul's judgment that the "minds [of the Jews are] hardened; for . . . to this day, whenever [the old covenant of] Moses is read a veil lies over their minds; but when a man turns to the Lord [i.e., the Christ] the veil is removed" (2 Cor 3:14–16). This alleged inability of the Jewish people to see eventually became construed in Christian theology as symptomatic of their willful ignorance, a notion responsible, in the history of art, for the motif of the synagogue's wearing a blindfold, a stereotype which powerfully determined perceptions by the Christian masses of Jews and Judaism throughout the Middle Ages and even into modern times. See especially W. S. Seiferth, *Synagogue and Church in the Middle Ages,* trans. L. Chadeayne and P. Gottwald (New York, 1970).

20. The completed production of the four gospels is dated by most New Testament scholars within the period of 70–100 c.e.

21. E.g., his being scornfully mocked by passers-by, and lots being cast for his garments.

22. Including *Jewish* scholars: cf. Isaac Troki, *Faith Strengthened,* repr. (New York, 1970); G. Sigal, *The Jew and the Christian Missionary: A Jewish Response to Missionary Christianity* (New York, 1981); D. Berger and M. Wyschogrod, *Jews and "Jewish Christianity"* (New York, 1978).

23. The terms are borrowed from *The Jesus Seminar: A Clarion Call to a Radical Reassessment of the Jesus Tradition* (brochure; May, 1985). When founded in 1985, the *Jesus Seminar,* comprising one-hundred ten scholars, asserted that

> drugstore books and magazines have too long played on the fears and ignorance of the uninformed. Radio and TV evangelists have traded in platitudes and pieties. Scholars, for their part, have limited their pronouncements to the classroom. . . . They have hesitated to broadcast the assured results of historical-critical scholarship out of fear of public controversy and political reprisal. But now some scholars have determined to quit the sanctuary of the study and classroom and go public. . . . This momentous move ["for the truth and its consequences"] calls for wide support.

24. Paraphrase of interview of Robert W. Funk in *Statesman-Journal* (Salem, Oregon; Saturday, April 5, 1986), p. 2c.

II.
THE PARTING OF THE WAYS:
ISSUES, PROBLEMS, CONSEQUENCES

The Parting of the Ways Reconsidered: Diversity in Judaism and Jewish-Christian Relations in the Roman Empire: "A Jewish Perspective"

Martha Himmelfarb

The story of how Jews and Christians went their separate ways so many centuries ago is of more than academic interest to all of us who are heirs to the western tradition. Whether we are Jews or Christians by conviction or by descent, this ancient parting continues to shape our understanding of ourselves. As the story has been told through the centuries by Christianity, the dominant culture, it is deeply anti-Jewish. Recently scholars have consciously attempted to eliminate its anti-Jewish elements, but too often these scholars, Jews as much as Christians, have been unable to break out of the categories set for them by the religious polemic they reject.[1] This inability is perhaps not surprising given how deeply the story is embedded in our views of the world. But the difficulty of the task is not an excuse for failing to make the effort. Here I hope to offer a few glimpses of quite different kinds of relations between Jews and Christians in the early centuries, relations that are perhaps unexpected from the perspective of later developments.

Let me start by attempting to sketch the picture of the parting of the ways current in scholarly literature. It looks something like this:

Jesus' followers, and thus the first Christians, were Jews. The earliest form of Christianity must be understood not merely against the background of contemporary Judaism, but as part of it, as one of the many *varieties* of Judaism in that period. I emphasize the term "vari-

47

eties." In the Second Temple period we need to speak, not of a single Judaism, but of varieties of Judaism.[2]

In those early days there was no reason why Christian Jews would have stood out. They differed from their neighbors on the identity of the Messiah and the fact of the Messiah's appearance in the world, but they agreed on many other issues, and they were certainly not the only group to hold positions that set them apart from other Jews to some extent. The book of Acts pictures Peter and the circle of Christians in Jerusalem worshiping daily in the Temple (3:46).[3]

Had Paul never appeared on the scene, the Jerusalem church, so Jewish in its piety, might have remained a variety of Judaism. But Paul's mission to the Gentiles radically altered the demographic balance of early Christianity against the Jerusalem community. By the late first century Christianity was primarily Gentile in its membership. What is more, Paul's mission to the Gentiles involved a rejection of the Torah. For the Jerusalem community, Jesus was the Messiah, but that in no way affected the continuing validity of the Torah. For Paul, the Torah had once been valid, but the Torah itself looked forward to the coming of Christ, who opened a new path to God. In the new age, the age in which Paul and his contemporaries lived, the Torah had become obsolete.[4]

Unlike the Christianity of the Jerusalem community, Paul's brand of Christianity, whether it was practiced by Jews or by Gentiles, could not be seen simply as a variety of Judaism. It was something new. As Paul's form of Gentile Christianity without Torah became the dominant form of Christianity, the separation of the daughter religion from its mother became inevitable.

The inevitable may have been given a push forward by the destruction of the Second Temple by the Romans. It has sometimes been suggested that even the Jerusalem community saw the destruction as punishment not simply for sin, a view many Jews held, but for the rejection of Jesus.[5]

It was also in response to the destruction of the Second Temple that the rabbis emerged as the new leaders of the Jewish people and began efforts to consolidate the past and adapt to the changed circumstances of the present.[6] Part of the attempt at consolidation involved repudiation of those who could no longer be accepted as members of the community of Israel, and it is at Yavneh, the new center granted Rabban Yohanan b. Zakkai by the Romans, that *birkat ha-minim,* the curse on Christians, was added to the eighteen benedictions, the central prayer of the Jewish liturgy. The addition of this curse to the prayer had the effect of driving

Jewish Christians out of the synagogues, for they were unwilling to curse themselves. At this time also the patriarch, the head of the Jewish community in Palestine recognized by the Romans, sent letters condemning Christianity to the Jewish communities of the diaspora. These letters contained a summary of Christian beliefs and a demand for excommunication of all who held them and perhaps also the text of *birkat ha-minim*.[7]

In the following centuries the relationship that had originally existed between Judaism and Christianity was reversed. From its origin as a small group within Judaism, Christianity became the fastest growing religion in the Roman Empire, and eventually the official religion, finding itself at last in a position to persecute the mother who had rejected it.

With the rise of rabbinic Judaism, Judaism stopped expanding. If the revolt against Rome from 66–73 did not finally destroy its appeal for non-Jews, the Bar Kokhba revolt of 132–35 surely did. Many Romans had once been attracted to Judaism, but the nationalism expressed in the revolts effectively brought an end to Gentile friendship for Judaism just as Christianity was beginning to offer itself as a serious alternative to the sensitive, searching pagan.[8]

By the middle of the second century, then, the fate of Judaism in western civilization was effectively sealed. The anti-Jewish measures of the Christian empire were still in the future, but they only enforced from outside the turn inward that the new Judaism of the rabbis had in fact chosen for itself. Judaism ceased to be the focus of Christian efforts to define a place in the world; instead, in the years before and after the Christianization of the empire, Christians were occupied by their attempt to come to terms with the great world of pagan culture.[9]

I trust that this picture sounds familiar. With its first stage, the understanding of earliest Christianity as a variety of Judaism, I have no quarrel. But from there on, despite its familiarity, questions can be raised at almost every point. The reading of Paul's message that forms part of the picture, a reading that has been in place almost since Paul wrote, has recently been challenged; John Gager discusses that challenge briefly in his essay in this volume.[10]

Recent scholarship has also shown that it is far from clear whether *birkat ha-minim* was in fact directed against Christians as such, or even against Jewish Christians. If the intent of the blessing was to exclude Christians from the synagogue, it failed. It failed in third-century Caesarea, where Origen preached on Sunday to Christians he knew were in synagogue the day before, and it failed in late fourth-century Antioch, where John Chrysostom condemned his flock for their visits to the synagogues at a time when the empire was already Christian. Even the existence of the letters condemning Christianity, to which some patristic sources seem to allude, is difficult to establish.[11]

The picture of rabbinic Judaism as inward looking and hostile to Gentiles is also open to criticism; it is clearly conditioned less by historical inquiry than by theology. Indeed, as I suggested above, this holds true for the whole of the story of the parting of the ways set out here. It is intimately related to Christian attitudes toward the Jews and Judaism as they have developed through history. Even those scholars who are consciously attempting to right the wrongs done in the traditional Christian picture have often allowed it to set the terms of the discussion.

But what I would like to discuss here is not any specific claim in the standard scholarly view of how Judaism and Christianity ultimately separated from each other, but rather the assumption implicit in that view that from some time late in the first century we need no longer concern ourselves with diversity in Judaism, an assumption that has profound implications for our understanding of Jewish-Christian relations. A good example of the reigning view of Judaism after the destruction of the Second Temple appears in an excellent recent discussion of early rabbinic attitudes toward Christianity. ". . . By the time Judaism and Christianity made their final break, it was the tannaitic[12] tradition which was almost completely representative of the Jewish community in Palestine and that segment of the Diaspora which remained loyal to its ancestral faith."[13] Our author feels no need to demonstrate this claim; he takes it as obvious, as do many students of the history of Judaism.

But is it true? Were almost all (note our author's good scholarly caution) of the Jews of Palestine and the diaspora rabbinic Jews during the period in which Christianity developed from a small Jewish group to the legal religion of the Roman Empire? The answer to this question, I believe, is an emphatic "no."

To begin with, it is inherently implausible that the rabbis could have imposed their form of Judaism on Jews all over the world in such a short space of time even with some limited backing from the Roman authorities. Further, recent scholarship has argued compellingly that the Mishnah, the first document of rabbinic Judaism, is a utopian document, not a practical book of law. The tannaim emerge in this reading as a small elite, describing the world not as it really was but as they wished it to be. Even in Palestine their influence was not widespread.[14] The archaeological evidence from Palestine and most strikingly from Dura Europos on the Euphrates, within the sphere of Babylonian Jewry, suggests that the rabbis were forced to tolerate much greater diversity among the Jews nominally under their leadership than most scholars had assumed or that they might have wished.[15]

Beyond this evidence for diversity within rabbinic Judaism, there is strong evidence to suggest that well into the period of the Roman Empire many Jews continued to live outside rabbinic influence altogether. Here I would like to treat two types of evidence for varieties of Judaism in the early rabbinic period, the archaeological evidence from the excavation of diaspora synagogues and the literary evidence of two pseudepigraphic texts.

Among the most important developments in the study of ancient Judaism in recent years is the discovery of several previously unknown diaspora synagogues.[16] By any standard the most spectacular of the finds is the huge and imposing synagogue at Sardis. Let me quote A. T. Kraabel's description of the synagogue:

> The first thing which strikes the visitor is the size and grandeur of the building, still inescapable today. The few other Diaspora synagogues which have been excavated are on the scale of a private dwelling; the scale of this building is that of the great gymnasium and Marble Court of which it is a part. . . . The space which the Jews had received was substantial, and they could have used it more "efficiently," had they wished, or had they been following practices known from other Diaspora synagogues. . . . The . . . Forecourt too is more attractive than efficient: there were sunlight and shade, splashing water [from a "municipally licensed fountain"[17]], brightly decorated floors and walls . . . , all in full view of anyone on his way from the Main Avenue to the gymnasium.[18]

As Kraabel's account indicates, this synagogue was not a freestanding building, but rather part of the enormous gymnasium complex built during the reconstruction of Sardis after the earthquake of 17 C.E. The building that became the synagogue was originally used for some other purpose. In order to turn it into a synagogue, the entrances to other parts of the complex were closed off so that the synagogue could be entered only from the street.[19] The use of the building as a synagogue dates to the third century C.E. at the latest.[20]

Who were the Jews of Sardis, owners of this impressive public space in a major Roman city? The first Jews arrived in Sardis at the time of the destruction of the First Temple.[21] The community grew during the third century B.C.E. as Antiochus III resettled a group of loyal Jews from his

Babylonian lands. Josephus reports a thriving community with considerable autonomy in the first century B.C.E. The city undertook to provide space for the Jews' liturgical needs, and the Jewish community faithfully contributed the annual half-shekel tax to the Jerusalem Temple and appears also to have been concerned about observance of the laws of kashrut.[22]

A flourishing Jewish community in a significant Roman town in the period before the rise of Christianity is nothing remarkable. But it appears that the importance of the Jews in Sardis, rather than declining in the period of the rise of Christianity, remained constant. Over eighty inscriptions have been uncovered in the Sardis synagogue, dating, like the use of the building as a synagogue, from the third century on. Of these inscriptions Kraabel writes,

> . . . They differ strikingly at one point from the hundreds of other Jewish inscriptions known from the Roman world. Elsewhere, for example at Rome, the texts may emphasize one's status within the *Jewish* community; the Sardis inscriptions stress rather the status of Jews outside the Jewish community, in the city and its government, and even beyond. Many donors proudly identify themselves as *Sardianoi*, "citizens of Sardis," and no less than nine may use the privileged title *bouleutes*, "member of the city council"; perhaps because of their wealth, the latter must have possessed considerable social status. In addition, three donors held positions in the provincial administration. . . .[23]

There is no evidence to suggest that the Jews of Sardis were influenced by the rabbis. The inscriptions, with two exceptions, are written in Greek, as is common in the diaspora. Rabbinic literature has little to say about Asia Minor in general,[24] and there is no evidence of any discontinuity between the Judaism of Sardis before the rise of the rabbis and after. These are all arguments from silence, but the burden of proof is surely on those who would wish to read the Sardis synagogue as rabbinic.

What can we say about the Judaism of the Sardis synagogue? Kraabel writes:

> For the understanding of Greco-Roman religions, Sardis presents us with an image of Jews and Judaism never as clearly attested before: still a minority, but a powerful, perhaps even wealthy one, of great antiquity in a major city of the Diaspora, controlling a huge and lavishly decorated structure on "Main Street." . . .[25]

> In view of its central location, its size, and its embellishments, it is hard to avoid the conclusion that the building was intended to be a showplace of Judaism for Sardis gentiles. . . . To passersby, it all must have said quite good things about Sardis Judaism; we believe that was by design.[26]

Literary evidence would, of course, provide us with a far more complete picture of the Judaism practiced in the synagogue of Sardis than archaeology alone can offer. To know what beyond the Bible constituted the religious literature of the Jews of Sardis, what they read and what they wrote, would allow us to achieve a new level of understanding. But it is a striking fact that Alexandria is the only city in the diaspora where Jewish literature of the post-biblical period can be located with any certainty, and even for Alexandria there is no clear evidence after the first century. It has been forcefully argued that 4-Maccabees comes from mid second-century Antioch.[27] That is about as close as we come to Sardis. Our evidence for Asia Minor, then, remains almost exclusively archaeological, and for Sardis at least we have no reason to complain.

At this point we might wish to ask how Christians fit into the picture of religious life in Sardis. What were the relations between the Jews of the Sardis synagogue and their Christian neighbors? Christianity in Sardis goes back to the first century, but its most famous representative is Melito, bishop of Sardis in the later second century. Melito's only surviving work is a sermon on the passion of Christ, *On the Passion,* which centers on the relationship between the passover of the Israelites in Egypt and the corresponding sacrifice of Christ, the Lamb of God.[28] The sermon is profoundly anti-Jewish. Christ's rejection and torture at the hands of the Jews is described in detail, and the Jews of Melito's time are called to account for it.

In the Middle Ages Christians polemicizing against the Jews saw the objects of their attack as an oppressed and downtrodden minority. The synagogue at Sardis shows us that the Jews must have appeared quite different to Melito. Melito himself was a member of an oppressed minority, and his theologically inspired hatred of sinful Israel who rejected God was surely fueled by the power and influence of the Jews of Sardis in his own day. Although Melito does not say so, the grandeur of the Sardis synagogue makes it likely that some of his flock were attracted to the synagogue, especially in light of the evidence for such visits from other locations. This, too, would surely have incensed the bishop.[29]

It is important to note the strength of Judaism relative to Christianity in Sardis in the later second century, because it is so often taken for granted that by this point Judaism was everywhere in retreat. When we remember that at this time Christianity was illegal and its practitioners liable to persecution, the relative influence in Sardis of the two religions should not be surprising. However, what could not have been guessed without the excavation of the synagogue, is that at Sardis Judaism did not retreat even in the face of the legalization of Christianity.

The Sardis synagogue is a basilica in plan; it would have made a fine church. The pattern of appropriating synagogues for use as churches was common in the period after the empire embraced Christianity. Yet the Sardis synagogue continued to function as a synagogue until 616 C.E., when the city was destroyed by the army of Chosroes II.[30] This point deserves emphasis: the Sardis synagogue remained a synagogue into the seventh century! Kraabel suggests that the remarkable strength of the Jews in Sardis even in the fourth, fifth, and sixth centuries may reflect pagan cooperation with the Jews against the common enemy, Christianity.[31] It is noteworthy that such cooperation could be successful in a town of some significance. The Sardis synagogue, then, may constitute evidence not only for the continued strength of Judaism, but also for the vitality of at least pockets of paganism well into the period of the Christianization of the empire.

The imposing synagogue of Sardis and the proud, prosperous Jewish community it represents stand alone among the remains of diaspora communities. But so few cities have been excavated that it is most difficult to judge what is typical.[32] As more evidence is uncovered Sardis may turn out to be less an exception than it now appears.[33] In any case it provides striking evidence that a form of diaspora Judaism with its own traditions and orientation toward the Gentile world did not disappear with the Second Temple.

Let me turn now to a second kind of evidence for varieties of Judaism in the early rabbinic period, the pseudepigrapha. "Pseudepigrapha" is the name given to a diverse body of Jewish and Christian works of the several centuries before and after the turn of the era attributed to heroes of the Hebrew Bible. These works take a variety of forms: apocalypses, testaments, narratives, poems. They represent a wide range of positions within Judaism and Christianity; as a group they have in common little more than the fact that their authors wrote under the names of great figures of the Hebrew Bible. It is frequently difficult to date these works with any precision or to locate them geographically. While some are indisputably Jewish, many contain a number of clearly Christian elements, and not infrequently it is difficult to decide whether a work was written by Jews and then reworked by Christians, or whether it was originally a Christian composition.

But here, instead of worrying about how to describe the relationship between Jewish and Christian elements in these works from a literary point of view, I would like to ask what the intertwining of these elements in two specific texts shows us about the varieties of relationships between Jews and Christians in our period.

3 Baruch, the Greek Apocalypse of Baruch, is a first-person account of the ascent to heaven of Baruch, the scribe of the prophet Jeremiah, after his lament over the fall of the First Temple to the Babylonians.[34] This setting allows the author to suggest a response to the crisis that is actually troubling his contemporaries, the fall of the Second Temple to the Romans. The work must date, then, to some time in the early rabbinic period. It is usually assumed that it was written in Egypt.[35] By the end of his tour of the heavens Baruch has received the comforting news that God in his heavenly temple will continue to forgive his people their sins even in the absence of the earthly temple. The work does not look forward to the restoration of the Jerusalem Temple, apparently because the universe can function quite well without it.

Despite one mention of "Jesus Christ, the Immanuel," and other less decisively Christian passages, 3 Baruch is widely considered to be a Jewish work. Those scholars who count it as such tend to treat the Christian elements as interpolations.[36] Others who take the Christian elements more seriously speak of a Christian editor or redactor of an earlier Jewish work or earlier Jewish traditions. Some even suggest that the work is originally Christian.[37]

Whoever is right, 3 Baruch is a very significant document for our discussion. If it is an originally Jewish work, 3 Baruch shows that there were Jews whose response to the destruction of the Second Temple was more like that of the Revelation of John than that of the rabbis. The rabbis would perhaps have agreed that life went on, but the author of 3 Baruch does not even hope to see the Temple restored. It is not surprising that a work like 3 Baruch would have appealed to Christians, who felt, as John of Patmos put it, that in God and his Lamb they had a substitute for the Temple. If we accept the view that 3 Baruch was originally a Jewish document, we have a Jewish author who viewed the destruction of the Temple in a way we associate with early Christians, and presumably a Jewish audience that shared his views. In the clearly Christian elements there is evidence for Christians who were perfectly willing to borrow from Jews, although they did feel called upon to make some improvements in the work they took over.

Even if 3 Baruch is from start to finish a Christian work, it sheds some interesting light not only on early Christianity, but also on contemporary Judaism. Why should a Christian author writing in Greek in the diaspora take the destruction of the Temple as significant? Why should he choose a hero of the Hebrew Bible to convey his message? The distance this author has traveled from Judaism does not appear very great. To what extent would the kind of Jewish community that was his point of reference have shared his attitudes? But the real point of 3 Baruch may be that our categories are inadequate. For the communities that read 3 Baruch, "Jewish" and "Christian" were apparently not mutually exclusive terms.[38]

My second example from the pseudepigrapha is 5 Ezra, a short Hebrew Bible. Whether the author of 5 Ezra was a Jew or a Christian, his work also shows that the ways are less decisively parted than the story as traditionally told would have us expect.

Was Judaism closed to outsiders from the time of the destruction of the Second Temple or of the Bar Kokhba revolt? Were all the Jews of the early rabbinic period rabbinic Jews? Did Judaism and Christianity go their separate ways once and for all sometime in the second century? Even this brief discussion of a few examples of the many possible kinds of evidence for varieties of Judaism in the Roman Empire should suffice to make us begin to doubt those givens.

In closing I would like to dwell for just a moment on the fact that the evidence considered in this essay was not transmitted by rabbinic Judaism. The pseudepigrapha were transmitted by Christians, primarily eastern Christians who stand at some remove from the mainstream of western Christianity that has formed our picture of Jewish-Christian relations.[41] The ruins at Sardis cannot be said to have been transmitted at all. Like Christianity, rabbinic Judaism needed to rewrite the past to define itself.[42]

As historians we take it for granted that we must be suspicious of any tradition's claims for itself. Historians have perhaps not been suspicious enough of the story rabbinic Judaism tells about its own emergence as the dominant form of Judaism in the Roman world. As historians, and perhaps not only as historians, we should also be suspicious of pictures of the prophetic discourse attributed to Ezra, the hero of the return from Babylonia after the exile.[39] It has been transmitted as an introduction to 4 Ezra, a Jewish apocalypse that uses the hero of the return to respond to the destruction of the Second Temple. On 5 Ezra there is near unanimity that we are dealing with a Christian work. The bulk of the work is Ezra's warning to the Jews that for their sins they are to be replaced by a new people. The work concludes with a vision of the Son of God on Mt. Zion handing out crowns and palms to the multitude of those who confessed him in this world.

Are these themes in themselves indisputable evidence for Christian authorship? It has recently been argued that they are not. God's son, the Messiah, appears on Mt. Zion surrounded by a multitude of people in 4 Ezra as well. The idea of God's anger with his own people even to the point of rejection is a commonplace of prophetic literature. So, too, is the idea of the salvation of other peoples.[40] It is certainly true that for early Christians, the combination of these themes was a crucial part of their self-definition, but were Christians the only ones to combine them?

Was the author of 5 Ezra a Jew or a Christian? To consider the question is to become aware of the difficulties involved in understanding what constituted Judaism and Christianity in our period. 5 Ezra shows clearly that a negative attitude toward the Jews does not preclude a profoundly Jewish outlook, which should come as no surprise to any one who has read the prophets of the past that make the past look much simpler than the present. As our experience today testifies, the existence of different kinds of Jews and Christians assures a variety of relationships between Jews and Christians. For the historian it is a worthy goal to show us a past as complex as the present.

NOTES

1. For a history of the discussion since World War II, see John G. Gager, *The Origins of Anti-Semitism: Attitudes Toward Judaism in Pagan and Christian Antiquity* (New York: Oxford, 1983), pp. 13–37. The single most important attempt at a fair treatment of the subject before World War II is James Parkes, *The Conflict of the Church and the Synagogue: A Study in the Origins of Antisemitism* (paperback ed.; New York: Athenaeum, 1969; first published 1934). Marcel Simon's *Verus Israel: A Study of the Relations between Christians and Jews in the Roman Empire (135–425)*, tr. H. McKeating from the 2nd French ed. of 1964 (New York: Oxford, 1986; 1st French ed., 1948) deserves special mention as a truly foundational work; while the influence of the old categories continues to be felt, it often succeeds in cutting through them.

2. Two excellent, non-technical works are Marcel Simon, *Jewish Sects at the Time of Jesus*, tr. James H. Farley (Philadelphia: Fortress, 1967), and Michael E. Stone, *Scriptures, Sects and Visions: A Profile of Judaism from Ezra to the Jewish Revolts* (Philadelphia: Fortress, 1980).

3. The literature on this subject is vast. See E. P. Sanders, *Jesus and Judaism* (Philadelphia: Fortress, 1985), for a recent presentation of the position that Jesus needs to be understood against the background of early Judaism. On the followers of Jesus, see, for example, Gerd Theissen, *The Sociology of Early Palestinian Christianity*, tr. John Bowden (Philadelphia: Fortress, 1978).

4. For a discussion of this picture of Paul's role in the context of an attempt at revision, see Gager, *Origins*, pp. 193–212.

5. Parkes, *Conflict*, p. 77.

6. See, for example, Jacob Neusner, *First Century Judaism in Crisis* (Nashville and New York: Abingdon, 1975). Neusner's more recent work takes a somewhat different stand, which will be discussed below.

7. This is the picture presented in Parkes, *Conflict*, pp. 77–81.

8. See, for example, Parkes, *Conflict*, p. 120, which admits that Judaism was still making converts in the second and third centuries, but only with difficulty.

9. See the observation of David Halperin in his review of E. P. Sanders et al., eds., *Jewish and Christian Self-Definition* (3 vols.; Philadelphia: Fortress, 1980–82), that the relationship of Christianity to Judaism receives very little attention in the volume on Christian self-definition (*Religious Studies Review* 11 [1985]:134). See also the comments of Robert L. Wilken in the preface to his *Judaism and the Early Christian Mind: A Study of Cyril of Alexandria's Exegesis and Theology* (New Haven and London: Yale, 1971), pp. ix–x.

10. This challenge originates with Lloyd Gaston. See his "Paul and the Torah," in Alan T. Davies, ed., *Antisemitism and the Foundations of Christianity* (New York, Ramsey, Toronto: Paulist, 1979); "Abraham and the Righteousness of God," *Horizons in Biblical Theology* 2 (1980): 39–68; and "Israel's Enemies in Pauline Theology," *New Testament Studies* 28 (1982): 400–23. See also Gager, *Origins*, pp. 193–264.

11. *Birkat ha-minim* and the letters: Reuven Kimelman, "*Birkat Ha-Minim* and the Lack of Evidence for an Anti-Christian Jewish Prayer in Late Antiquity," in E. P. Sanders, ed., with A. I. Baumgarten and Alan Mendelson, *Jewish and Christian Self-Definition: Vol. 2, Aspects of Judaism in the Greco-Roman Period* (Philadelphia: Fortress, 1981).

Origen: Selecta on Exodus 12:46 (*Patrologia Graeca* XII.285–88), Homilies on Leviticus V.8 (*Patrologia Graeca* XII.459); and N. R. M. de Lange, *Origen and the Jews: Studies in Jewish-Christian Relations in Third-Century Palestine* (Cambridge: Cambridge University, 1976), p. 86.

John Chrysostom: *St. John Chrysostom: Discourses Against Judaizing Christians*, tr. and ed., Paul W. Harkins (The Fathers of the Church 68; Baltimore: Catholic University of America, 1979); and Robert L. Wilken, *John Chrysostom and the Jews: Rhetoric and Reality in the Late Fourth Century* (Berkeley and London: University of California, 1983).

12. The tannaim are the rabbis of the first and second centuries.

13. Lawrence H. Schiffman, "At the Crossroads: Tannaitic Perspectives on the Jewish-Christian Schism," in Sanders, ed., *Self-Definition* 2:115.

14. See Jacob Neusner, *Judaism: The Evidence of the Mishnah* (Chicago and London: University of Chicago, 1981), esp. pp. 1–5.

15. See the brief discussion in Kraabel, "The Diaspora Synagogue: Archaeological and Epigraphic Evidence Since Sukenik," *Aufstieg und Niedergang der römischen Welt* II 19.1 (1979): 477–83, and the references there.

16. My debt to the work of A. T. Kraabel, who has done so much to make historians of ancient Judaism aware of the evidence of these synagogues and their significance will be evident in the notes below.

17. Kraabel, "Impact of the Discovery of the Sardis Synagogue," in G. M. A. Hanfmann, ed., *Sardis from Prehistoric to Roman Times: Results of the Archaeological Exploration of Sardis 1958–1975* (Cambridge, Ma.: Harvard University, 1983), p. 184.

18. Ibid., p. 188.

19. Kraabel, "Diaspora Synagogue," 485.

20. Kraabel, *Sardis*, p. 179.

21. Ibid., 178–79. "Sepharad" in Obadiah 20 is the Hebrew name for Sardis.

22. Kraabel,. *Sardis*, p. 179. Josephus, *Jewish Antiquities* 16.171, 14.261.

23. *Sardis*, p. 184.

24. Ibid., p. 183.

25. "Diaspora Synagogue," pp. 487–88.

26. *Sardis*, p. 188.

27. André Dupont-Sommer, *Le quatrième livre des Machabées* (Bibliothèque de l'école des hautes études, sciences historiques et philologiques, 274; Paris: Honoré Champion, 1939), pp. 67–85.

28. For the text with English translation and introduction, Campbell Bonner, ed., *The Homily on the Passion by Melito Bishop of Sardis and Some Fragments of the Apocryphal Ezekiel* (Studies and Documents 12; London: Christophers, and Philadelphia: University of Pennsylvania, 1940).

29. For a detailed discussion of the factors involved in Melito's attitude toward the Jews including his quartodecimanism, see Kraabel, "Melito the Bishop and the Synagogue at Sardis: Text and Context," in David Gordon Mitten, John Griffiths Pedley, and Jane Ayer Scott, eds., *Studies Presented to George M. A. Hanfmann* (Fogg Art Museum. Harvard University Monographs in Art and Archaeology II; Mainz: Philipp von Zabern, 1971), pp. 77–85. See also "Sardis," pp. 186–88.

30. Kraabel, *Sardis*, pp. 179–80; "Diaspora Synagogue," 488.

31. Kraabel, *Sardis*, p. 186.

32. Kraabel's summary article, "Diaspora Synagogue," treats all of the dias-

pora synagogues known as of its writing; there are seven, of which one bears a question mark.

33. See Kraabel's comments on Aphrodisias, *Sardis,* p. 181.

34. An English translation of 3 Baruch by H. E. Gaylord, Jr., can be found in James H. Charlesworth, ed., *The Old Testament Pseudepigrapha* (Garden City: Doubleday, 1983) 1:653–79.

35. The grounds for this assumption are not very strong; they include affinities to another apocalypse, 2 Enoch, which is usually placed in Egypt, and the figures of mixed animal and human form that are taken as characteristically Egyptian. See George W. E. Nickelsburg, *Jewish Literature between the Bible and the Mishnah* (Philadelphia: Fortress, 1981), p. 303, and John J. Collins, *The Apocalyptic Imagination: An Introduction to the Jewish Matrix of Christianity* (New York: Crossroad, 1984), p. 198.

36. See, for example, Nickelsburg, *Jewish Literature,* p. 300, and Collins, *Apocalyptic Imagination,* pp. 198–99.

37. On the range of positions, see Gaylord in Charlesworth, *Pseudepigrapha* 1:655–56.

38. See the comments ibid., 1:656.

39. For an English translation, see any edition of the Apocrypha, in which 5 Ezra appears as 2 Esdras 1–2. To add to the confusion, the work that appears in the Apocrypha as 2 Esdras is referred to by scholars as 4 Ezra. Thus 5 Ezra is also 4 Ezra 1–2.

40. Robert A. Kraft, "Towards Assessing the Latin Text of '5 Ezra': The 'Christian Connection,' " in George W. E. Nickelsburg, ed., with George W. MacRae, *Christians Among Jews and Gentiles: Essays in Honor of Krister Stendahl on His Sixty-fifth Birthday* (Philadelphia: Fortress, 1986), pp. 158–69. Kraft's argument is concerned with the relationship between the two families of texts and treats the themes mentioned above only briefly (esp. pp. 162–67). These questions are discussed in greater detail in a dissertation in progress by Theodore Bergren of the University of Pennsylvania. An abstract of a paper by Bergren entitled "Judging Christian Authorship in the Pseudepigrapha: The Case of 5 Ezra (4 Ezra 1–2)" appears in *Abstracts* for the American Academy of Religion/Society of Biblical Literature 1986 Annual Meeting. Despite his agreement with many of the points Kraft makes, Bergren still inclines to a view of 5 Ezra as Christian (private communication, May 12, 1986).

41. Even 5 Ezra, which comes down to us in Latin, is generally believed to have been translated from Greek.

42. This essay has been deeply influenced by Walter Bauer's seminal work, *Orthodoxy and Heresy in Earliest Christianity,* English tr. from the 2nd German ed. of 1964, Robert A. Kraft and Gerhard Krodel, eds. (Philadelphia: Fortress, 1971; German 1st ed., 1934). Bauer argued that "orthodox" Christianity came to dominate the scene only rather late, after it had succeeded in overcoming a wide variety of opposing streams with equal or better claims to antiquity,

and that it did so by a conscious process of propaganda and suppression that leaves us with only traces of a vast body of ancient literature. The particulars of the situation for Judaism in the early centuries of this era are quite different, but a study of Judaism in the Roman world inspired by Bauer would surely bear fruit.

The Parting of the Ways:
A View from the Perspective
of Early Christianity: "A Christian
Perspective"

John G. Gager

Among historians of early Christianity it has been customary to argue that relations between Christianity and Judaism in the first two to three hundred years of the common era fall neatly into two distinct and virtually non-overlapping phases:

—in the first phase, the Jesus movement must be understood and treated as a reform or revitalization movement entirely within Judaism of that time: the members of the movement were Jews; they proclaimed Jesus as the long-expected Messiah of Israel; their Bible was the Hebrew scriptures; their mission was limited primarily to other Jews; they continued to worship in the Temple at Jerusalem for as long as it stood; and they continued to observe the Mosaic covenant in every aspect of their lives. In short, nothing about the early movement would justify placing it outside the boundaries of first-century Judaism—so much so in fact that we cannot even speak of Jewish influences on the Jesus movement, because the very notion of influence presupposes something that stands outside. This first phase lasted for a period of several decades following the death of Jesus and came to an end somewhere in the 60s and 70s of the first century.
— according to the traditional view, the second phase of Christianity's development began with Paul and accelerated rapidly after the col-

lapse of the Jewish revolt against Rome in the year 70. At this point, the Jesus movement shifted away from Judaism and pushed outward into the broader Roman Empire. It is in this double process of expansion and transformation that it became "Christianity," i.e., a religion not only distinct from Judaism but cut off from all future contact. The classic statement of this second phase appears in the work of Dom Gregory Dix and has been repeated many times by many others: "After the year 70, there were no relations between Jews and Christians except hostile ones."[1]

As the development of Christianity outside of Palestine becomes the focus of attention in the second phase, the traditional view is forced to come to terms with the fact that ancient Judaism was not limited geographically to Palestine. Indeed, wherever Christians turned outside Palestine, they encountered well-established Jewish communities, many of which had been in existence for centuries before the birth of Christianity. The normal practice at this point is to assert that Christians and Jews had no positive relations with one another in these non-Palestinian settings. The two biblical faiths simply parted company, each one denying the validity of the other and erecting impenetrable walls in between. And as if to underline the finality and inevitability of this split, a further series of claims is made about the religious or cultural status of Judaism in the broader Greco-Roman world:

1. Jewish communities lived in a condition of self-conscious isolation from their Gentile neighbors and from the political, social and cultural life of the Greco-Roman world in general.[2] Their synagogues were not open to Gentiles nor were Jews interested in spreading Judaism to them. Certainly there was nothing like a Jewish missionary attitude or activity.
2. In line with this, it follows that Judaism was without appeal to outsiders. Given its peculiar customs, its rigid monotheism and its attitude of isolationism, it was simply not an attractive religious option for Gentiles.
3. Few Gentiles were attracted to Judaism; the reason usually given is that the prevalent attitude of Gentiles toward Judaism was one of hostility.[3] Those Gentiles who somehow became associated with synagogues were quickly won over to Christianity. The evidence most commonly cited here is the book of Acts where on almost every occasion when Christian missionaries proclaim the Christian message

in synagogue communities, the pattern of response is that Jews reject the message whereas the Gentile God-fearers—that is, those Gentiles already associated with synagogues but not full converts—embrace it enthusiastically and immediately.[4]

4. After the appearance of Christianity in the Roman world, Gentiles were drawn exclusively to the Christian faith; Judaism was left even more isolated than before. And, as if to complete this isolation, synagogues soon enacted a ban on Christian participation, making it impossible for followers of Jesus to have any form of association with them.[5] From that point on there were no relations between Jews and Christians except hostile ones.

Such is the picture of Jewish-Christian relations that has come down to us—not just in the writings of the New Testament but also in scholarly books and articles as well as more popular forms of literature. To what I have already said about the individual elements of this picture, I would only add the following: each of the elements is interdependent on the others; they reinforce one another. Conversely, once one begins to question any one of them, all of them threaten to crumble!

By now it should be apparent that I judge this traditional picture to be one-sided and distorted. Despite occasional exceptions, it is still fair to say that this picture has been the center of attention for the better part of almost two thousand years. Obviously, it will not be possible to undo the effects of two thousand years of bad history in a single stroke. What I can do is point to a few areas where this history has been particularly distorted, to indicate how it might be possible to rethink some of the essential elements in it, and to spend a little time trying to indicate how such bad history came to be written in the first place and why it was believed for so long in the face of contradictory evidence.

Let me begin with the central notion that there was a final break between Judaism and Christianity somewhere between 70 and 150 C.E. In her article in this volume, Martha Himmelfarb has shown how problematic the idea is from what we know of Judaism during this period. Sadly, the evidence to support the idea of such a break is just as weak when we look at it from the Christian side. In general, when scholars make such a claim they base their arguments on two kinds of evidence: individual New Testament writings on the one side and the overall shape of the New Testament on the other side. Certainly the general impression given by the New Testament as a whole is unfavorable to Judaism—and as I will try to show, deliberately so. Among individual writings, the most important have probably been the book of Acts and the letters of Paul. I will have more to say about the book of Acts a little later, but for the time being let me just indicate that the story told by its author is determined more by theology than by an effort to create what we might call objective history. Thus, when we read repeatedly that Jews consistently rejected the Christian message while Gentiles already associated with synagogues embraced it unanimously, there is good reason to believe that what is being expressed here is the author's belief that Gentiles loyal to Christ have replaced Jews as the chosen people of God. No doubt many Jews in the ancient world were disturbed when they found Christian missionaries preaching a crucified Messiah and the abrogation of the Torah in their synagogues. But at the same time, we know full well that those Jews who followed Jesus without abrogating the Torah did not disappear from the scene in the 40s, even though Acts has them disappear from the story shortly after Paul's appearance in chapter 11.

A somewhat different approach must be taken to Paul, as we encounter him in his own letters in the New Testament. According to the dominant reading of Paul, he insisted on a radical break between Judaism and Christianity—Gentiles replace Jews as the chosen people of God, and faith in Christ replaces and cancels God's revelation to Israel in the Torah. The result of this reading has been that Paul emerges as the great theologian and architect of the final break. Although there is much to say about this endlessly fascinating figure, let me simply indicate that I am more and more convinced that the traditional reading of him is wrong. Not only are there virtually no texts in his letters that can be made to square with this view of Pauline triumphalism; not only are there numerous texts where Paul specifically repudiates the notion that Gentiles have replaced Jews in God's plans, but the entire edifice of this interpretation is made possible only by giving totally non-contextual readings of his letters. What I am saying here is that if we pay close attention to Paul's audience and those against whom he is arguing, we realize that all of his apparently negative judgments about the Torah are directed, not against Jews or at their relationship to Torah, but instead against other *Christian* missionaries.[6] These missionaries, whom we meet repeatedly in Paul's letters, followed him from one location to another, preaching a radically different gospel. According to them, any Gentile who followed Jesus had to undergo circumcision and follow the Mosaic commandments.[7] In short, they had to become Jews. For Paul, this message flew in the face of his own preaching that in Christ God had done something dramatically new for Gentiles by opening a path to righteousness apart from—but not against—the Mosaic covenant. Thus every one of his arguments is directed, not against Jews or Judaism, but against these counter-missionaries who, as Paul saw it, wanted to undo God's work. For him, circumcision and the Mosaic covenant were indeed no longer applicable—but only for Gentiles.

These are radical ideas and I do not expect them to find a ready hearing. The real point I want to make is that the old reading of Paul, the position that would have him proclaiming God's rejection of Israel, is made possible only by ignoring the immediate and specific context of his letters. It is a very short step, but one full of momentous consequences, to forget to whom Paul is talking and what particular circumstances he is addressing. If we take this step, if we ignore these circumstances, if we forget that he is addressing himself to highly localized conditions and dilemmas of the first century, then our reading of Paul's arguments will certainly lead us to the mistaken conclusion that they are directed, not against internal Christian opponents, but against Judaism itself.

Ironically, what made this mistaken reading of Paul just about inevitable was the incorporation of his letters into the new scriptures of early Christianity, the New Testament. What is more, the process of creating the New Testament as Christian scripture took place not in the first or the early second century, when the individual writings were composed, but in the second, third and fourth centuries, when they were selected and put together as a collection. And by that time two important changes had taken place: first, the circumstances so common in the mid-first century, with widely differing views of the status of Gentiles competing openly for dominance within the Christian movement, were no longer in effect; and second, official Christianity found itself regularly and searchingly criticized by official Judaism. The most common form of this criticism was that Christianity's claim to be the new and true Israel lacked validity because Christians had abandoned the traditional practices associated with the Mosaic covenant. Not surprisingly, the Christian response to these criticisms took the form of the counter-argument that the Mosaic covenant had been superseded by Christ and, in line with this, that Christians had replaced Jews as the true biblical people.

These were the conditions under which the New Testament was created, with Paul's letters at its very center. Moreover, these conditions are clearly reflected in the overall shape and message of the New Testament, a shape and message not of the first century but of the second, third and fourth centuries. My point here is simply that under these conditions it was almost inevitable that his arguments would be read as they have been ever since. The enemy, so to speak, was no longer to be found within the camp, in the form of anti-Pauline Christian missionaries; the enemy was now outside, in the form of Judaism. And what more natural than to assume that Paul should have been arguing against the enemy of that later time, namely, Judaism itself. Once that assumption was made, there was nothing to prevent Paul from being read as the theologian of Christianity's triumph over Judaism and the architect of the final parting of the ways.

What I have argued thus far is that we cannot read the New Testament—or its individual writings—as if they provide a full or unambiguous account of relations between Christians and Jews in the early centuries of the common era. We have seen that the official story of Christianity's encounter with Judaism has stressed one voice in a much wider conversation—in this case the voice of harsh criticism and rejection. The New Testament represents the views of the winners in a long series of ancient debates about Judaism *within* the Christian community. We must be careful not to confuse the retrospective, value-laden story told by the winners with the much more complex picture that is now beginning to emerge. In particular, it is now possible to state with assurance that the assumption of a parting of the ways somewhere between 70 and 150 is true only for what we may call the official leadership within Christian circles. It is most certainly not true for many ordinary Christians who did not share the view that loyalty to Jesus meant breaking all contacts with Jews or repudiating the religious validity of their faith.

In other words, I want to advance the proposition that for many Christians, there was no break at all with Judaism—not in 70, not in 150, indeed not even in 370, some three hundred years after virtually all previous scholars have told us that the final break took place. I could point to all sorts of evidence to illustrate this assertion. I could cite the rulings of various ecclesiastical councils in the fourth century in which bishops forbid Christians to have their fields blessed by rabbis and charge Christians not to celebrate Passover in Jewish homes.[8] I could mention the fact that in the third and fourth centuries, Christian writers ranging from North Africa in the west to Syria in the east, write about Christians who were practicing circumcision, celebrating Jewish festivals and regularly attending Jewish synagogues.[9] Or I could move in a somewhat different direction by reinforcing Martha Himmelfarb's picture of Judaism's continued appeal among Gentiles long after Christianity has supposedly replaced Judaism as the only biblical faith either interested in or open to Gentiles.

Instead, let me turn to the greatest Christian city in the ancient world—the city of Antioch.[10] To make the case even more difficult, I propose that we look at relations between Christians and Jews in Antioch, not in the second century, when Christianity was still a struggling minority, but in the late fourth century, more than fifty years after the death of the first Christian emperor. For our source, we will choose John Chrysostom, one of the most influential figures in his own time and for centuries thereafter.[11] In the 380s, John was a presbyter in Antioch and already famous as a preacher. During these years, John preached a series of sermons that has usually been called "Against the Jews."[12] The problem with this label is that it is just accurate enough to be completely misleading. In fact, the sermons are really about Gentile Christians in John's church who were actively involved with local synagogues—not as converts to Judaism or as apostates from Christianity, but alongside their continued membership in the church. In particular, we learn from the sermons that these Christians were in the habit of honoring the major Jewish holidays of the fall season—the New Year, Yom Kippur, and Sukkoth—which is exactly the time of year when John delivered his sermons. But if these Christian Judaizers are the immediate targets of his wrath, Judaism and Jews are the ultimate victims. What I mean by this is that John's technique in trying to dissuade the Christian Judaizers from what he regards as their foolish ways is to denigrate Judaism in every way possible. He compares the synagogue to a theater (1.2;4.7.3) and a brothel (1.3.1); he tells his listeners that it is better to die of fever than to be healed in a synagogue (8.7). Of the Jews themselves, he literally shouts that they have degenerated to the level of dogs (1.2.2); they are drunkards and gluttons (8.1); they are ignorant of God (6.4.7); their festivals are worthless and their synagogues are dwelling places of demons (1.6.2–8). "What else do you wish me to tell you?" he concludes in one of the sermons. "Shall I tell you of their plundering, their covetousness, their abandonment of the poor, their thefts, their cheating in trade? The whole day long will not be enough to give you an account of these things" (1.7.1).

Now what, you might ask, could have prompted such an outburst from John? What activities caused such outrage? And at a deeper level, why did the involvement of Christians with Judaism lead him to assault Judaism in this way, or to say, as he does in other places, that he hates the Jews and has come to lust for combat with them (6.1.2)?

We have already seen that certain members of his congregation made a regular practice of participating in important festivals of the

Jewish year. In addition, John tells us that these Christians made a regular practice of swearing oaths in the synagogues (1.3.5) and of using them as places for medical cures (8.5.6)—like an ancient counterpart to Lourdes and other sites of pilgrimage and healing in later Christianity. In John's own words, they had a high regard for the Jews and they honored the synagogue as a holy place (1.3.1). We also know that we are not dealing with an insignificant minority of Christians, for John refers to them on several occasions as numerous and he warns the congregation not to speak of their numbers in public.

What are we to make of all this? I trust that at least some of you share my sense that what we learn about the Christian Judaizers from John's sermons is not a little disturbing. It is disturbing in the first instance because it fits so poorly with what all of us have been taught about the final parting of the ways. It is disturbing also because it now turns out that for some Christians and for some Jews, relations remained open and active late in the fourth century and well beyond, as Martha Himmelfarb has shown. How, we might ask, does this fit with the picture in the book of Acts according to which Gentiles literally fled from the synagogues when Christianity appeared on the scene? How does this fit with what we learn from Sardis[13] and other major cities where Gentiles—both pagan and Christian—continued to find power and piety in synagogues for centuries after Judaism had supposedly collapsed into itself and chosen the path of isolation and hostility toward the surrounding world? How are we to judge the Judaizing Christians in Antioch, whom we can now place in an unbroken line of tradition that reaches back to the very beginnings of the Christian movement? And finally, how are we to assimilate the obvious willingness of synagogues to accept Gentiles—both pagan and Christian—as in some sense members of their religious community?

In raising these questions, I do not mean to convey the impression that conflict and confrontation were absent in relations between Judaism and Christianity in these centuries. We need only read John Chrysostom's sermons to remind ourselves that this was not the case. What I *am* suggesting is that we are now in a much better position to put these conflicts and confrontations into their proper historical and religious perspective. Specifically, we can now see, not just that there were other voices in the dialogue, but that the hostile voices are directly linked to these other voices, that the hostility arises not so much from external confrontations between Christians and Jews as from an *internal* Christian debate regarding the proper understanding of Judaism itself. To use somewhat different terms, all of the surviving evidence suggests that the continued vitality of Judaism provoked profound internal divisions among Christians. The real debate was never between Christians and Jews but among Christians. The real problem was not outside but within. Eventually, as we know, the anti-Jewish side won out and its ideology became normative for subsequent western history. But today, for the first time in many centuries, we are able to hear both—or rather, all sides of that debate. And for religious traditions that define themselves in historical terms, these new voices in that ancient debate must be of some significance.

By way of trying to sum up my argument that the final parting of the ways between Judaism and Christianity did not take place as or when we have been accustomed to think about it, I would like to raise the question of what this new picture means for traditional explanations of Christian anti-Judaism. What I mean by this question is that assertions about the final parting of the ways have always been accompanied by explanations of what it was that led Christianity not just to part company with Judaism but in the process to repudiate and denigrate Judaism itself. In other words, from the Christian perspective, the parting of the ways always involved a theological dismissal of Judaism. And the question is, Why should this have been the case? Why was it necessary not just to leave Judaism but to dismiss it as well? Or, to turn the question around, why was it not possible for Christianity simply to go one way while allowing Judaism to follow another?

Answers to these questions have been put forward by historians, sociologists, theologians and even psychiatrists. I confess that I have made use of them myself. But I have much less confidence in them now than I did even a short time ago. Let me examine a few of them in order to make plain what I mean. One explanation holds that competition between religious communities—or competition of any kind for that matter—leads to tension and antagonism, especially on the part of the loser. Certainly in John Chrysostom's case, we can see that he looked upon the Judaizing members of his congregation as lost to the faith. But competition does not always breed contempt, so that a second factor has sometimes been introduced by those who look at conflict from a sociological point of view. Here the claim is made that no conflict is ever as deep or intense as when it involves closely related groups. As one sociologist has put it: "The closer the conflict, the more intense the conflict."[14] And there can be no doubt that Judaism and Christianity were close to each other in many ways. Both sought sole possession of the Hebrew scriptures; both insisted on the sole claim to represent the true Israel; and both sought recognition among outsiders as the sole bearer of biblical revelation. On these issues, which lay at the very heart of both traditions, other sociologists have insisted that we must take with great seriousness the fact of Judaism's continued existence and vitality as a threat to what we might call the symbolic universe of early Christianity—in other words, the appeal of Judaism not only to pagans but to Christians as well did not fit well with Christian triumphalism. What this means is that "an alternative symbolic universe poses a threat because its very existence demonstrates that one's own universe is less than inevitable."[15] Under these conditions, as Peter Berger has put it rather ominously, the threatened party may seek to reinforce its legitimacy through the process of what he calls conceptual nihilation, or in slightly different language, through the theological liquidation of whatever appears to threaten its own universe.[16] This, I take it, is what Rosemary Ruether has in mind in *Faith and Fratricide,* when she concludes that for "Christianity, anti-Judaism was not merely a defense against attack, but an intrinsic need of Christian self-affirmation."[17]

As I have already indicated, I count myself among those who have found these explanations helpful in understanding the underlying forces that moved Christianity toward a parting of the ways with Judaism. But it should be apparent to others, as it has become apparent to me, that there is a fundamental difficulty in fitting these explanations into the main thrust of my observations in this paper. For if some Christians did not part company, but instead resisted efforts from ecclesiastical leaders to force them to do so, then we can no longer apply these explanations across the board to all Christians. They may still be useful in understanding the motives and emotions of those who undertook to defend the legitimacy of Christianity by the conceptual nihilation of Judaism, but for many others such explanations will not do for the simple reason that there is nothing to explain. Or, to put it somewhat differently, it is wrong to argue, as Ruether has done, that anti-Judaism is intrinsic and inevitable for Christian self-affirmation.

In short, the hostility that characterizes much of early Christian literature on Judaism does not tell the full story—though it does tell the official one. My general impression is that the dividing line between those who saw no need to repudiate Judaism in affirming their Christianity and those who did tends to follow the contours of power and authority within early Christian circles. As we might expect—and here we can find plenty of parallels in our own world—those in positions of power often define and defend themselves by emphasizing the differences between *us* and *them*. It is the additional factor of power and authority, I think, that turns competitors into enemies and insists on the conceptual nihilation of competing systems.

But among early Christians of an ordinary sort, many seem to have experienced no difficulty in combining allegiance to Jesus with a respect for Judaism that sometimes took the form of direct participation in the life of the synagogue. Ultimately, we might even say inevitably, those in positions of power and authority won out. And in the process they painted a depressingly negative picture of their opponents—in this case of Jews and of those whom we might call the Christian friends of Judaism. All of us, I fear, have been victimized by the consequences of their victory. But at the same time, as I have tried to argue in this paper, that victory need not be final. For all of us it may still be possible—many centuries after the initial victory—to hear the full debate and to decide for ourselves who the winners are and who the losers.

NOTES

1. "The Ministry in the Early Church," in *The Apostolic Ministry,* ed. K. E. Kirk (London, 1946) p. 228.

2. See, for example, W. H. C. Frend, *Martyrdom and Persecution in the Early Church* (Garden City, N.Y., 1967) p. 96.

3. See the extended discussion in J. G. Gager, *The Origins of Anti-Semitism: Attitudes Toward Judaism in Pagan and Christian Antiquity* (New York, 1983) pp. 35–112.

4. See now A. T. Kraabel, "Greeks, Jews, and Lutherans in the Middle Half of Acts," in *Christians among Jews and Gentiles: Essays in Honor of Krister Stendahl* (Philadelphia, 1986) pp. 147–157, and J. G. Gager, "Jews, Gentiles, and Synagogues in the Book of Acts," in the same volume, pp. 91–99.

5. For a new and challenging interpretation of this much-discussed issue, see R. Kimelman, "*Birkat Ha-Minim* and the Lack of Evidence for an Anti-Christian Jewish Prayer in Late Antiquity," in *Jewish and Christian Self-Definition,* vol. 2: *Aspects of Judaism in the Greco-Roman World,* ed. E. P. Sanders (Philadelphia, 1981) pp. 226–244.

6. On these questions there is a growing body of literature; see especially Lloyd Gaston, "Paul and the Torah," in *Antisemitism and the Foundations of Christianity,* ed. A. T. Davies (New York, 1979) pp. 48–71, and J. G. Gager, *Origins of Anti-Semitism,* pp. 113–264.

7. So also, for example, the members of the Jesus movement from Jerusalem who insisted that "those who were not circumcised in accordance with Mosaic practice could not be saved" (Acts 15.1).

8. See the old but still valuable discussion of James Parkes, *The Conflict of*

the Church and the Synagogue: A Study in the Origins of Antisemitism (New York, 1961), pp. 174–177.

9. In general on this and related subjects, see M. Simon, *Verus Israel: A Study of the Relations between Christians and Jews in the Roman Empire (135–425)* (New York, 1986).

10. See W. Meeks and R. Wilken, *Jews and Christians in Antioch in the First Four Centuries of the Common Era* (Missoula, Montana, 1978).

11. See now R. Wilken, *John Chrysostom and the Jews* (Berkeley, California, 1983).

12. Now available in English; see *Saint John Chrysostom: Discourses Against Judaizing Christians,* translated by Paul W. Harkins; The Fathers of the Church, vol. 68 (Washington, D.C., 1979).

13. On Judaism in Sardis see the literature cited in the article of Martha Himmelfarb.

14. L. Coser, *The Functions of Social Conflict* (New York, 1956), p. 70.

15. P. Berger and T. Luckmann, *The Social Construction of Reality* (New York, 1967) p. 38. Compare the words of John Chrysostom, which offer a remarkable illustration of this general principle: "If the Jewish ceremonies are venerable and great, ours are lies. But if ours are true, as they are true, theirs are filled with deceit" (1.6.5)

16. Ibid. p. 159.

17. *Faith and Fratricide* (New York, 1974) p. 181.

III.
MEDIEVAL DEVELOPMENTS
INSTITUTIONALIZING TENSIONS AND
CONFLICTS

Medieval Jews on Christianity: Polemical Strategies and Theological Defense

Jeremy Cohen

Writing nearly a century ago, the noted Anglo-Jewish scholar, Solomon Schechter, exclaimed with regard to the texts of medieval religious polemic: "I do not think that there is in the whole domain of literature less profitable reading."[1] The records of religious controversies between medieval Jews and Christians are fraught with problems for the historian, and they understandably grate against the sentiments of contemporary Jews and Christians in search of mutual cooperation and understanding. One cannot readily expect them to reflect accurately the doctrinal subtleties of the theological issues under discussion or the particulars of the actual confrontations between spokesmen for the opposing faiths. These liabilities of polemical literature notwithstanding, the present generation of historians has begun to confront it with greater sensitivity to its assets: its importance in—and hence its ability to illuminate—the ongoing dialectic between Judaism and Christianity, as well as its tendency to mirror numerous features of the historical setting in which that conflict ensued.

It is from such a perspective on the value of these polemical works for their modern readers that this paper will consider several medieval Jewish attacks on Christianity. One should recall that animosities between Christians and Jews increased and intensified during the Middle Ages, to the extent that by the sixteenth century, Christian rulers had expelled their Jewish subjects from England, France, Spain, Portugal, Sicily, Southern Italy, and sizeable portions of Germany. Along the way, numerous Jewish communities had been massacred, most had been subjected to increasingly severe forms of political exploitation and legal discrimination, and virtually all had encountered the popular conception of the Jew as agent of Satan—expressed in the infamous blood libel, ritual murder and well-poisoning charges, and *Judensau* motif in Christian art. These developments obviously fueled the hatred of the Jews for the Christian population in whose midst they lived, which hardly served to mitigate the intensity of their problem.

Nevertheless, while the hatred between the two religious communities was certainly mutual and often expressed itself in a like manner, polemics developed and took shape differently within each group, responding to markedly dissimilar sets of final causes. To appreciate the singular character of Jewish anti-Christian polemic, therefore, one must first examine the development and salient features of the medieval Christian attack on Judaism.

Before it became social or economic, anti-Judaism among Christians was doctrinal. From relatively early on in the history of the church—certainly by the time of the conversion of Constantine—the *adversus Judaeos* tradition in Christian apologetics constituted a cornerstone of Christian theology. For Christianity to be right, Judaism had to be wrong; on a fundamental level, they were mutually exclusive. The admonition of St. John Chrysostom in late fourth-century Antioch speaks directly to this point:

> Where Christ-killers gather, the cross is ridiculed, God blasphemed, the father unacknowledged, the son insulted, the grace of the Spirit rejected. . . . If the Jewish rites are holy and venerable, our way of life must be false. But if our way is true, as indeed it is, theirs is fraudulent. I am not speaking of the Scriptures. Far from it! For they lead one to Christ. I am speaking of their present impiety and madness.[2]

Even in the absence of Jews or of a threat from the Jewish community, important churchmen of both patristic and medieval periods asserted the validity of their theology in terms of a negation of Judaism. Social, economic, and political factors—e.g., competition in the marketplace, moneylending, incipient nationalism—added greatly to anti-Jewish animus during the high and later Middle Ages, but it is difficult to imagine that European Christendom would have expelled nearly all of its Jews without theological impetus and justification. These crystallized gradually in the twelfth, thirteenth, and fourteenth centuries, stemming from a heightened awareness of the beliefs and practices of medieval rabbinic Judaism which led Christendom to perceive the Jew as unsuited for further toleration.

Perhaps one can thus distinguish three periods in the evolution of medieval anti-Jewish polemic.[3]

(1) The *adversus Judaeos* expositions of the early Middle Ages, intended primarily to reinforce the faith of Christians, typically comprised "a stereotyped enumeration of proofs taken from the Bible for the truth of Christianity, and the detection of prophecies and prefigurations that were enriched from the present status of the Jews in 'servitude' and dispersion."[4] That Christian theologians employed anti-Jewish polemic above all to assert the truth of Christianity to a Christian audience points to an anomalous but significant aspect of their writings. Despite their virulence, the primarily theological and pedagogic motives of the polemics resulted in their characterization of the Jew as the stereotypical representation of the Old Testament, and not in accordance with historical reality. Judaism embodied the decadent, obsolete covenant of the letter, the law, and the flesh—all that Christianity had supplanted and replaced. No matter that the patristic era also witnessed the heyday of classical rabbinic Judaism and the compilation of the Talmud, processes of intensive cultural vitality and creativity that enabled Judaism to survive the destruction of the Temple and the loss of a national center in Palestine. From the perspective of the Church Fathers, as Augustine proclaimed, the Jews "have remained stationary in useless antiquity."[5] Christian theology insisted that they did, and that Judaism had stopped developing, giving way to Christianity on the day of Jesus' crucifixion. The ambivalence, whereby the church needed Judaism in order to divest it through polemic of its biblical covenant and election—to cite Beryl Smalley's metaphor—"had built a [characterological] prison for the Jewish people."[6] But the testimonial purpose served by the Jews insured their preservation and survival; for the time being, the Church had no need to convert them, and it officially forbade all forms of anti-Jewish violence.

(2) Beginning in the twelfth century—owing to the Crusades, the growth of medieval cities, and the cultural revival which they fostered—there appeared a heightened sensitivity to the growing presence of European Jewry. A large number of more aggressive anti-Jewish treatises reflected greater contact, concern, and conversation with a thriving Jewish community which did not quite appear the fossil of antiquity that earlier Christians insisted it had to be.

(3) In the thirteenth century, the position that medieval Jews no longer had a rightful place in a properly ordered Christian society finally emerged. The church had awakened to the existence and nature of talmudic, postbiblical Judaism, which demonstrated that Jewish history did not end on the day of Jesus' death. Yet in good medieval fashion, it deduced not that its forebears had misunderstood, but that contemporary, rabbinic Jews had forsaken their allegiance to the Old Testament—the didactic function which had insured their inclusion in Christendom. Like unorthodox Christians, these "heretical" Jews became the rightful objects of efforts to convert, to persecute, and to exclude.

In marked contrast to this concern of the church for the Jews and their religion, medieval Jews had relatively little doctrinal interest in Christianity and its teachings. As soon as the early church had left the Jewish community, it had ceased to represent a major threat, comprising just another Gentile group whose coexistence with the Jews caused them no *theological* difficulty. The early medieval Jewish folktales about Jesus and his followers that have been grouped under the title *Toledot Yeshu* therefore compliment Peter and Paul for taking a misguided belief in Jesus out of the Jewish community and into the Gentile world.[7] When removed from real contact with Christians and its concomitant dangers, Jews did not have much reason to polemicize against Christianity. Medieval Jewish anti-Christian polemic developed almost completely *in response* to Christian anti-Judaism, as I shall attempt to demonstrate with respect to several noteworthy rabbinic works.

Inasmuch as the *adversus Judaeos* arguments of the early Middle Ages did not pose an immediate threat to the security of the Jews, the latter saw little need to respond to them and thereby to engage Christians in polemical disputes. Rabbinic homilists, historians, and poets certainly viewed Christian Rome and Byzantium as epitomizing the contemporary oppressor of Israel, perhaps ranking as the third or fourth of the four kingdoms in Daniel's eschatological prophecies. The extent to which such ideas were polemical—and not simply historiographical—stands in direct proportion to the extent that their proponents held the church responsible for their misery. The scornful portrayal of Jesus in the Talmud, Midrash, and *Toledot Yeshu* bespeaks an entirely negative opinion of Christianity's origins and worth, but it, too, developed entirely within the Jewish community and folklore, with no specific, identifiable external stimulus. Simply put, the development of Jewish anti-Christian polemic paralleled that of Christian anti-Jewish polemic: until the Crusades, it was primarily an in-house affair. In the eleventh century, to be sure, one finds the great Jewish exegete, RaShI (Rabbi Solomon ben Isaac of Troyes, 1040–1105) warning his readers of various dangers confronting the Jews in European Christendom, and refuting christological interpretations of biblical prophecies. On Isaiah 9:5–6, for instance, which relates that "a son has been given us and authority has settled on his shoulders," RaShI decries the exegesis of the Christian "heretics" (*minim*) who apply the verse to "their error"—i.e., Jesus—because Isaiah refers to a contemporary figure, and "didn't that 'error' not come until five hundred years later?" Yet even though RaShI foreshadowed a new era, neither he nor any other western Jew before him felt impelled to compose an anti-Christian tract, the numerous patristic and early medieval works *adversus Judaeos* notwithstanding.

Only the emergence of the second phase of Christian polemic as listed above induced Jews, beginning in the twelfth century, to compose entire treatises in response. Jacob ben Reuben's *Milḥamot ha-Shem* (*Wars of the Lord*), Joseph Kimḥi's *Sefer ha-Berit* (*The Book of the Covenant*), and Joseph Official's *Sefer Yosef ha-Meqanne* (*The Book of Joseph the Zealot*) all exemplify this early brand of Jewish polemic. A particularly instructive work of this genre is the anonymous *Sefer Nizzaḥon Yashan* (*Nizzaḥon Vetus*), a late thirteenth or early fourteenth-century anthology of polemical arguments from the previous two hundred years, and one of the most revealing polemics of its type. It boldly defends Judaism against the attacks of increasingly aware Christian opponents and strikes out at Christianity as well. Like the Christian polemic to which it responds, its focus remains almost entirely biblical. Organized according to the order of the biblical canon, it proceeds through the passages of the Hebrew Bible interpreted christologically by the church, and those of the New Testament susceptible to attack by the Jews. A representative paragraph addresses the christological and trinitarian exegesis of the famous words of Genesis 1:26,

"Let us make man." The heretics say that "Let us make" implies two, and they are father and son. You can put off such a heretic by answering: Indeed, the matter is as you say. The father told the son, "My son, help me, and let you and I make man." However, the son rebelled and did not wish to help his father, and so the father made man alone without the son's help, as it is written, "And God created man," with a singular rather than a plural verb. Consequently, the father became angry with his son and said, "If the time should come when you need my assistance, I shall not help you just as you have not helped me." So when the day came for the son to be stoned and hanged, he cried out in a bitter voice, "My Lord, my Lord, why have you forsaken me? Why are you so far from saving me . . . ?" and he begged for his help [Mt 27:46]. Then the father told him, "When I asked you to help me make man, you rebelled against me and did not come to the aid of the Lord, and so my own power availed me and I made him without you. Now you too help yourself, for I shall not come to your aid."[8]

The Jewish polemic thus reflects the increased contact between Jews and Christians, offering substantive and strategic advice for disputing with clerics, and referring to debates between particular rabbis and churchmen. Attesting to disturbing developments in Christendom's treatment of European Jewry, the *Nizzahon Yashan* refutes the blood libel, sharply denounces Jews who convert to Christianity, and decries the attack of the church on the Talmud. Yet in a variety of ways, just like the Christian polemic it opposes, it manifests a period of transition. While the church was beginning to turn its sights on *contemporary* Jews, the Jewish polemicist still felt secure enough to denounce Christianity and contemporary Christians in the strongest, most vituperative language. Not Jesus, nor his mother, nor his ancient followers, nor the Catholic clergy escaped the most scathing rebuke. Just as the twelfth and early thirteenth-century church did not quite know how to resolve the inconsistencies in its Jewish policy, so the *Nizzahon Yashan* cares little for the logical coherence of its polemic and considerably more for countering all conceivable Christian arguments, at every twist and turn of a disputation. If our author frequently discards christological exegesis because it deserts the historical context of Hebrew scripture, he still will interpret prophetic rebuke in the Bible as applying to Christians of postbiblical times. And just as Christians of his time have turned to the study of biblical and rabbinic works with new interest and vigor, so the *Nizzahon Yashan* is well acquainted with the New Testament, various patristic writings, and rites and practices of the high medieval church. At times it will even provide the Latin or German for a text or issue under discussion, so that Jewish disputants can address their opponents on their own terms. Much of the distinctive tone and forensic methodology of the work is conveyed in a passage like this:

> The heretics criticize us in connection with the *Beichte* for not confessing the way they do, and they cite proof from the book of Proverbs: "He that covers his sins shall not prosper, but he who confesses and forsakes them shall have mercy [Prov 28:13]. This is how you should

answer him: On the contrary, one should conceal one's sins from another man and not tell him, "This is how I have sinned," lest the listener be tempted to commit that sin. One should, rather, confess one's sins to God. . . . The nations of the world . . . conceal their sins from God, for adultery, fornication, and murder are found among them. In fact, all the commandments that God ordained are hidden among them, for they concoct different interpretations so that they can change such commandments as circumcision, the prohibition of swine, suet, and blood, indeed, all the prohibitions in the Torah. Not only that, it was because of the fact that they wallow in fornication and yet their Torah forbade them from marrying that they agreed to require men to come and tell their sin and publicize their adultery so that they might know which women are having extramarital affairs. They then tell those women that they would like to do the same, and the women cannot deny anything because the adulterer has already identified them. This is certainly the explanation, because otherwise why doesn't the pope, who is regarded as the vicar of their God and who has the power to forbid and permit, give nuns the authority to hear the confession of women? It would clearly be more proper and acceptable . . . so that they would not be seduced into fornication and adultery.[9]

As such, the *Nizzaḥon Yashan* is expressive of a Jewish community concerned by the rising intensity of Christian polemic, but whose author has not sensed a change either in the basic ecclesiastical policy of tolerating the Jews, or in the polemic which supported such a policy.

The thirteenth century saw the onset of the third phase of Christian polemic as a result of the singular efforts of Dominican and Franciscan friars to regiment and police many facets of European cultural life. The friars charged that medieval Jews had forsaken the Old Testament religion, which had hitherto justified their preservation in Christian society, for the "heretical" ways and beliefs of the Talmud. Therefore, so ran the argument, Christendom ought no longer to permit them or their religious rites to remain. Called to defend his adherence to rabbinic Judaism before the king of Aragon and his Dominican advisors in 1263, the noted Rabbi Moses ben Naḥman (Naḥmanides) subsequently published a polemical account of his famous Disputation of Barcelona with the former Jew, Friar Pablo Christiani.[10] Although by no means favorable to the Christians, Naḥmanides' pamphlet reveals the growing frustrations of the Jews as they tried to respond to the friars' new arguments. No longer was the polemic confined to the exegesis of scripture. Rather,

Pablo now cited directly from works of rabbinic literature in support of his claims

> (1) that the messiah, which means Christ, whom the Jews have been awaiting, has undoubtedly come; (2) that the said messiah, as had been prophesied, should at once be divine and human; (3) that he in fact suffered and died for the salvation of the human race; [and] (4) that the legal or ceremonial [provisions of the Old Testament] terminated and were supposed to terminate after the arrival of the said messiah.[11]

The suggestive rabbinic homilies (or *aggadot*) adduced by Pablo put Naḥmanides in a quandary: Accepting the rabbinic texts adduced by Pablo meant admitting that the Messiah, who was both human and divine, had already come and suffered and died in order to redeem mankind. Refusing to accept Pablo's evidence, however, amounted to rejecting the authority of rabbinic tradition—hardly an option for a practicing Jew. Nor could the rabbi remain silent; for the focus of the polemic had shifted from Christianity's claim to have fulfilled biblical prophecies to the orthodoxy of rabbinic Judaism and its outspoken contemporary representatives—in particular, Naḥmanides himself.

The themes of the rabbi's polemical pamphlet underscore the precarious and delicate nature of his situation. First, in conformity with most rabbinic polemicists who had preceded him, Naḥmanides appealed to the context of the sources adduced to validate Christianity; Naḥmanides had not rejected rabbinic texts, but Pablo had misunderstood them. The texts in question did not in fact refer to the Messiah, as Pablo assumed they did; they alluded to the birth of the Messiah but not to the messianic redemption, or they could not possibly refer to Jesus.

Herein lay the second noteworthy tendency in Naḥmanides' polemic: an attempt to return the debate from its consideration of rabbinic sources to an evaluation of Christianity. The rabbi repeatedly strove to demonstrate a lack of conformity between Pablo's messianic *aggadot* and the life of Jesus. In a lengthy speech, delivered in an effort to halt the discussion of Jewish beliefs and to deal exclusively with Jesus himself, Naḥmanides proclaimed to King James of Aragon that the question of the Messiah was not the key issue separating Jews and Christians. The Messiah, argued the rabbi, will be a king just like James, different only insofar as he will enforce Jewish law in his kingdom. Noting that the observance of Jewish law in a Christian kingdom demands much greater self-sacrifice—and therefore yields much greater reward—Naḥmanides quipped that King James was thus worth more to him than the Messiah. Rather, the doctrine of the incarnation comprised the crucial point of contention between church and synagogue. "That the creator of heaven and earth . . . should become a fetus in the womb of a certain Jewess, grow there for seven months, be born an infant, then grow up, and later be delivered into the hands of his enemies, that they should condemn him to death and execute him, and that afterwards . . . he lived and returned to his previous abode—the mind of no Jew nor of any other man will accept this."[12] Given this problem, why should Naḥmanides and Pablo bother themselves with a debate on the Messiah? Yet Naḥmanides failed to revise the agenda for the disputation. Insisting that Naḥmanides remain on the defensive, the friars refused to submit Christian theology to debate.

Third, Naḥmanides defended the contemporary, rabbinic Jewish way of life, for which he stood, as the faithful, literal application of the Mosaic precepts—not as a heretical departure therefrom—while he downplayed the authority of the midrashic texts cited by his opponent. Compelled to reject several homilies outright, Naḥmanides elaborated:

> Friar Pablo asked me if the messiah of whom the prophets have spoken has already come, and I said that he has not come. So he [Friar Pablo] adduced an aggadic work in which it is said that on the very day of the temple's destruction the messiah was born. And I stated that I do not believe this. . . . You should know that we have three categories of writings: One is the Bible, and we all believe in it unquestioningly. The second is called Talmud, and it is a commentary on the commandments in the Torah; for in the Torah there are 613 commandments, and not one is left unexplained in the Talmud. And we believe it [the Talmud] in its interpretation of the commandments. We have yet a third class of writing called midrash, that is to say homiletic literature (*sermones*), like that produced if the bishop were to rise and deliver a sermon and one of those listening were to like it and write it down. As for this class of writing, if anyone believes it, it is fine, and if anyone does not believe it, no harm is done.[13]

This line of argument, however, threatened to play directly into the hands of the Dominicans. A noted champion of the Aggadah during the recent Maimonidean Controversy, could Naḥmanides credibly disclaim responsibility for its teachings? The only level on which the rabbi could respond decisively was a fourth—that of *ad hominem* attack on his opponent: Just as Pablo sought to depict his rival as one who had abandoned the religion of the Bible for a talmudic perversion thereof, so too Naḥmanides denounced the friar as renegade and apostate from his faith.

> Are you the clever Jew that discovered this novel interpretation and apostasized because of it? Are you the one who proposes to the king to gather the Jewish scholars for you, so that you can debate with them concerning the novel interpretations you have found? Have we never heard of this matter before now? There is not a monk or child who will not pose this question to the Jews! This question is ancient indeed.[14]

The proper contrast lay not between Naḥmanides and true Judaism but between Pablo and the true intentions of the Talmud. Of the classical rabbis Naḥmanides inquired,

> Why did they not apostasize and turn to the religion of Jesus as has done Friar Pablo, who has understood from their words that the faith of the Christians is the true one—God forbid!—and has gone and apostasized on the basis of what they said? Yet they and their disciples who received the law directly from them lived and died as Jews, just as we are today. . . . For if they believed in Jesus and his religious teaching, why did they not do as has done Friar Pablo, who understands their words better than they themselves?[15]

Naḥmanides' Hebrew polemic manifests important changes in the history of medieval Jewish-Christian polemic. Traditional modes of argumentation now failed to put Christianity on the defensive, and rabbis struggled hard to identify and define the issues so that they could respond effectively and in kind. Fear of shortchanging medieval rabbinic Judaism on the one hand, coupled with the fear of overly inciting the presiding Christian authorities on the other, dominates Naḥmanides' attempt to vindicate his allegiance to postbiblical, talmudic Judaism.

By the end of the fourteenth century, meager hope remained for medieval European Jewry, as the logic of the friars' polemical ideology was being implemented. Expelled from England and France, the Jews encountered new waves of hostility and violence in Spain which induced thousands to convert to Christianity, many of whom intended to continue living as Jews in secret. Perhaps numbering among these *conversos,* Isaac ben Moses ha-Levi (Profiat) Duran authored several attacks on Christianity, the most extensive of which was his *Kelimat ha-Goyim* (*The Shame of the Gentiles*). The unrestrained tone of Duran's indictment of Christianity bespeaks the desperation of the Jewish community; little more could be lost by antagonizing a Christian audience. Yet the substance of Duran's polemic is also noteworthy. He proceeded methodically through most of the major tenets of medieval Christian theology—the divinity of Christ, the Trinity, the virgin birth, the incarnation, original sin, the obsolescence of the law, the efficacy of the sacraments, the primacy of Rome, and the authority of Jerome's Vulgate—and adduced copious references to New Testament texts. In each case, argued Duran, neither Jesus nor his disciples ever dreamed of the doctrines which the Catholic Church upholds. Duran labeled the earliest Christians *to'im*, errant ones—ignorant, pitiful, perhaps even demented, but ultimately well-intentioned (*ḥasidim shotim*); he referred to Mark 12:28–30 to show that Jesus misquoted even the famous *Shema' Yisra'el*/"Hear O Israel" prayer [for the Vulgate reads "Dominus Deus tuus," "the Lord your God" instead of "the Lord our God" as in Deuteronomy 6.4], which every traditional Jew learns as a toddler. "See how this poor wretch didn't even know the *Shema' Yisra'el*," mocked Duran.[16] Later patristic and scholastic theologians, however, Duran dubbed *mat'im* (those who beguile, who cause error) "for in their delusion they have reached the point of deceiving a great multitude—and this inasmuch as they have dabbled in philosophy, have intended to draw on an 'enemy' (i.e., true reason) in upholding their faith, and have thus crafted a concoction of honey and bitter wormwood."[17] Yitzhak Baer and Frank Talmage have offered the intriguing suggestion that writing only a century before the beginning of the Reformation, Duran thus echoed the voices of noteworthy Christian critics of the late medieval church—e.g., Marsilius of Padua, William of Ockham, and John of Paris, among others.[18] Granting the likelihood of this assertion, I would add that as Duran displayed familiarity with an impressive array of Catholic writers—including Augustine, Peter Lombard, Aquinas, Vincent of Beauvais, and Nicholas of Lyra—he charged medieval Christians with precisely the same "heresy" of which the friars had accused rabbinic Jews: abandoning the classical teachings of scripture (in this case the New Testament) for institutional and doctrinal corruption. Even from a Christian point of view, he argued, the authority of such a religion was illegitimate.

No modern student of medieval Jewish-Christian relations should fail to be struck and disheartened by their steady deterioration, even as European civilization was passing through some of its most creative centuries. As one seeks to analyze and interpret the various accusations which each religious group hurled at the other, it is instructive to note that Jews consistently responded to Christian hatred in kind, while the stimuli which gave rise to their polemic remained different. Lacking a modern education in psychoanalysis, anthropology, and the phenomenology of religion, Jewish rabbis and philosophers of the Middle Ages surely considered the distinctive beliefs of Christianity absurd. And yet, especially in their status as an alien minority, they had little commitment to the vision of a world in which everyone would think like them, longing merely for one in which they could think and do as they pleased. Harsh and unkind though their indictment of Christianity may have been, medieval Jews polemicized against Christianity to defend their community, not to propagate their faith.

NOTES

1. Solomon Schechter, *Studies in Judaism* (New York, 1896), p. 104.
2. *Against the Jews,* Homily 1, trans. in Wayne A. Meeks and Robert L. Wilken, *Jews and Christians in Antioch in the First Four Centuries of the Common Era,* Society for Biblical Literature, Sources for Biblical Study 13 (Missoula, Mont., 1978), p. 97.
3. I have presented and defended this schema at great length in *The Friars and the Jews: The Evolution of Medieval Anti-Judaism* (Ithaca, 1982), and, most recently, in "Scholarship and Intolerance in the Medieval Academy: The Study and Evaluation of Judaism in European Christendom," *American Historical Review* 91 (1986), 592–613.
4. Amos Funkenstein, "Basic Types of Christian Anti-Jewish Polemics in the Later Middle Ages," *Viator* 2 (1971): 373–375.
5. *Tractatus adversus Judaeos, PL* 42:51–67.
6. Beryl Smalley, *The Study of the Bible in the Middle Ages,* 3rd. ed. (Oxford, 1983), pp. 25–26.
7. Samuel Krauss, *Das Leben Jesu nach jüdischen Quellen* (1902; repr. Hildesheim, 1977); Günter Schlichting, *Ein jüdisches Leben Jesu: Die verschollene Toledot-Jesu-Fassung Tam u-mu'ad,* Wissenschaftliche Untersuchungen zum Neuen Testament 24 (Tübingen, 1982).
8. David Berger, *The Jewish-Christian Debate in the High Middle Ages: A Critical Edition of the Nizzahon Vetus,* Judaica: Texts and Translations 4 (Philadelphia, 1979), 43 (= Heb. pp. 4–5).
9. Ibid., 223 (= Heb. p. 158).
10. The following account reviews the major arguments presented in *The Friars and the Jews,* pp. 108–122.
11. Yitzhak Baer, "The Disputations of R. Yechiel of Paris and of Nachmanides [Hebrew]," *Tarbiz* 2 (1931):185.

12. Moses ben Naḥman, *Kitvei ha-RaMBaN,* ed. Charles B. Chavel, 2 vols. (Jerusalem, 1963), 1:310–11.

13. Ibid., 1:308.

14. Ibid., 1:317.

15. Ibid., 1:303–304.

16. Profiat Duran, *The Polemical Writings: The Reproach of the Gentiles and "Be Not Like unto Thy Fathers"* [Hebrew], ed. Frank Talmage, "Kuntresim:" Texts and Studies 55 (Jerusalem, 1981), 53.

17. Ibid., 4.

18. Ibid., xvi–xix; Yitzhak Baer, *A History of the Jews in Christian Spain,* trans. Louis Schoffman *et al.,* 2 vols. (Philadelphia, 1961–66), 2:150–58, 474–75.

Persons and Their Institutions: Medieval Popes and Jews

Edward A. Synan, F.R.S.C.

Many scholars, some few saints, and even a few drudges, who with some reason might be termed "scholastics," work in our time on a most exacting enterprise, an effort to recover the truth about the ways in which medieval Christians came to terms with the ancient People of God, the Jews. Thus it was not only assonance that recommended these terms to the very distinguished interlocutor who chose them to designate his contribution to the session on "Institutionalizing the Tensions and Conflicts."*

The thirteenth-century European Jewish community faced both a multifaceted institutional environment—papacy, empire, kings, prince-bishops, friars, monks, and universities—and also the strong personalities who directed (and were directed by) those institutions. Popes acted within the traditions of "the papacy" and theologians within the conventions of university theology; mendicant friars, thanks to papal approval, cut across the normal ecclesiastical frontiers.

A sobering reflection on the very posing of our problem in terms of "institutions" is that medievals with a philosophical bent, whether Jews, Christians, or Muslims, found what they termed "the universal" an endlessly troubling intellectual phenomenon. What, if anything, does a common noun name? To what reality or realities in the world of experience does "Judaism" or "Christianity" or "Islam" refer? Although we speak and think about general issues thanks to our capacity to contrive universal terms—"triangle," "human being," "Jew," "pope"—to match our equally universal notions, the world (it is generally conceded) is made up of singulars, of individuals. We may think and speak of "Judaism," but we meet only Jews; one thinks and speaks of "Christianity" or of "the papacy," but the first must be reduced to a mass of persons with all their various characteristics who share the Christian faith in some intelligible way, and the second designates a file of individuals, nearly all of whom were endowed with strong personalities.

Put another way, the historian may be torn between the necessity for economy and intelligibility of discourse that makes us speak of groups or institutions and, on the other hand, a countervailing necessity to speak of the real individuals in whom those groups or institutions have their being.

We are apt to think of persons as "good" and of institutions as "bad." Individual rights against Leviathan: state, church, army, lynch mob—those rights have our sympathy from the beginning. Is there a solution to this dichotomy? Here an analysis will be made that tends to show another way of posing our question, a way in which persons and their institutions can be reconciled, both poles respected.

Two Jewish scholars (who may well be saints, but would hardly thank us for calling them "scholastics") provide concrete evidence of how one of these two poles, the individual and the institution, can command research in our field.

Before examining these two programmatic emphases (to say nothing of an observation by a third scholar which must count as yet another methodological direction) we shall do well to make a rapid survey of how medieval popes and Jews experienced each other. The thousand years between Pope Gelasius I, the first pope who exhibits a documented Jewish policy, and Pope Alexander VI, elected to the papacy at the moment of the great Spanish expulsion of Jews and Muslims, were a time of neither unrelieved hostility, nor of unmarred amity. Although rapid, this survey demands a modicum of documentation. Since the papal documents are in Latin, my translations will be controlled in every case by the original text. These documents demonstrate to what Jefferson called "a candid world" that Catholic Christianity (the great Reform postdates our period) has no inescapable anti-Judaism built into its structure. Despite the strictures of some modern scholars, whether Christians or Jews or unbelievers, neither the Christian perception of Jesus as Messiah, his condemnation by Pilate and Sanhedrin notwithstanding, nor the conception that Christians of Gentile origin need not observe halachic precepts, entail hostility toward the kith and kin of Jesus. Many a Christian failed, and alas, still fails to see this—as we have failed on the whole gamut of Christian faith and morals. In great part our popes have transcended the generality of Christians on this front as well as on so many others.

Still, one must be prepared to see worked out in the documentation of this ecclesial history a number of melancholy facts: Our world needs redemption indeed; we are a community of wayfarers, not the blessed of the world to come. We are right to pray that the kingdom come and quickly; the church is right to take the fundamental sinfulness of our race from the beginning as her point of departure. In short, neither a sweeping condemnation of Christians, and least of all the popes, as doctrinaire enemies of the Jews, nor total exoneration of all Christians in fixing responsibility for unspeakable injustice to the Jews in the name of faith, can survive the evidence.

MEDIEVAL POPES; MEDIEVAL JEWS

It is heartening to be able to report that Pope Gelasius I (492–496) intervened with a brother bishop in favor of a Jewish friend:

> A very distinguished man from Telesia, although he may appear to be of the Jewish persuasion, has so striven to make himself approved by Us that We ought by rights to call him one of Our own; he has made a special plea in behalf of his parent, Antonius, with the result that We must commend him to Your Charity. And thus it is fitting, Brother, that you should so conduct yourself with respect to the aforesaid, in deference to Our will and Our commands, that not only should he in no way suffer oppression, but rather, in whatever way may be neces-sary for him, he should rejoice in the assistance of Your Charity.[1]

The words "although he may appear to be of the Jewish persuasion" juxtaposed with the pope's conviction that he ought to call the man from Telesia "one of Our own" exclude the possibility that Gelasius referred to a convert from Judaism, a situation so often invoked when a papal intervention to save a "Jew" during the horrors of the Holocaust is mentioned. Hitler, of course, was hardly inclined to count a converted Jew anything but a Jew; Gelasius could not have used the turn of phrase he employed had he been writing of one who had accepted baptism.

With Gelasius, too, began the perennial dialectic between papal protection of Jewish rights and papal repression of illegalities by Jews. This is apparent in his discreet instruction to church authorities that they investigate the claim of a slave that he had been circumcised by a Jewish master even though the slave had been a Christian from infancy. Pope Gelasius wished neither the Christian "religion dishonored," *religio temerata,* nor "a lying slave" contending against the legal rights of his master, *competentis iura domini* to flout the laws. Let the appropriate authority, Gelasius ordered, "faithfully examine the truth of these matters."[2]

Concern with protecting the human and religious rights of the Jews in Christendom and a simultaneous concern to maintain the prestige and influence of the church was well-formulated by Pope Gregory the Great (590–604). Responding to a complaint he had received from the Jews of Cagliari to the effect that a convert from Judaism to Christianity had broken into a synagogue on Easter Sunday along with rowdy companions and there had deposited a number of Christian symbols (his baptismal robe for one), the pope invoked the Christianized civil law, undoubtedly the Theodosian Code 16, 8, 27; in Gregory's words:

> As the determination of Law does not permit Jews to erect new synagogues, so also does it permit them to possess their old ones without disquietude.[3]

Against the new Christian and his henchmen the pope had a pastoral observation which would be the classic papal stance on conversion to the Christian faith in the future:

> Let them not answer that they have done this thing out of zeal for the faith . . . they ought to realize that they must rather use restraint so that through them one might be drawn to choose, not to reject, and also that the unwilling are not to be compelled. . . .[4]

A complaint from the Jewish congregation in Palermo occasioned the formula in Gregory's response from which would grow by successive additions the later "Constitution for the Jews":

> Just as license ought not to be presumed for the Jews to do anything in their synagogues beyond what is permitted by law, so in those points conceded to them, they ought to suffer nothing prejudicial.[5]

Pope Gregory joined to the respect for the persons and the freedoms of Jews so evident in the texts cited, a multifaceted conversionist policy that by our standards hardly squares with those texts. He recommended reducing the tasks of prospective converts, a lightening of their tax burdens, pensions, the abbreviation of the normal catechumenate, and free baptismal robes for the poor among them.[6] Despite the faint air of bribery inherent in these concessions, Gregory and his successors in the papacy without exception opposed forced baptism, an outrage that Gregory knew was not rare:

> . . . many Jews in those regions have been led to the baptismal font by force rather than by preaching. . . . With them the sermon is what must be used . . . and may God lead to the rebirth of a new life as many of them as He grants.[7]

Here, of course, is a distant anticipation of the conversionist sermons with the forced attendance of Jews so much resented in the high Middle Ages. Still, papal opposition to brute force made its way into general church legislation, notably into the *Decretum* of Gratian,[8] a twelfth-century compilation that perdured with many additions until the codification of canon law during the years of the First World War; in a letter to the Patriarch of Constantinople Gregory wrote:

> Your Fraternity knows well what the canons say concerning bishops who wish to be feared for their blows: We have been constituted shepherds, not persecutors. . . . A novelty, indeed a thing unheard of, is this doctrine that extorts faith through blows![9]

A later canonist would explain, however, once a Jew had been baptized, provided force had been less than "absolute," that convert could not evade the penalties of heresy should Christian norms be abandoned.[10] Thus was the consistent prohibition by popes of forced baptism eroded.

Conversion could, and occasionally did, run in the opposite direction. No instance of a medieval Christian's turn to Judaism is better documented than that of the German deacon Bodo. Despite his Christian education, his pilgrimage to Rome, and his entrée to the royal palace, Bodo and a nephew of his passed over to the Jewish community at Saragossa. Bodo became a soldier, married a Jewess, and changed his name to Eleazar.[11] A Spanish Christian chronicler asserted that he stirred up Muslims against Christians to the point of using force to compel conversion either to Islam or to Judaism.[12] Fear of anti-Christian pressure, whether from Jews or from Muslims was acute, and not only in

Spain. A Roman synod in the reign of Pope Gregory VII (1073–1085) forbade King Alphonso VI of Spain to permit "Jews . . . to be lords over Christians or to wield any power over them."[13] Legislation of this type would reach its apogee in the Fourth Lateran Council of 1215 under Pope Innocent III (1198–1217); it looked back to the Roman Law of Christian Emperors. Jewish masters must permit their Christian slaves the practice of their religion;[14] should such slaves be circumcised their freedom was granted immediately and later legislation made the circumcision of slaves a capital offense.

Finally, simply to buy a Christian slave earned a Jewish master confiscation.[15] The Fourth Lateran Council went further yet in specifying the restrictions imposed upon Jews in Christendom. Economic disabilities included restraints against "immoderate usuries," the continuation of tithes on formerly Christian property after title had passed over to Jewish owners,[16] distinctive dress for Jews and Saracens in Christian lands,[17] a blanket prohibition of public office-holding by Jews[18] and, under the color of protecting public order, a prohibition of public festivities and even of appearing in public during the solemn days of the Christian holy week.[19] With this onerous legislation the situation of Jews in medieval Christendom was given its definitive structure. As we shall see, the popes were to honor both sides of the equation: Jewish survival on one side, but the repression of whatever might wear the guise of anti-Christian influence; and Jewish leadership would periodically call upon the reigning pope for protection when Jewish welfare was threatened.[20]

Still, social reality is never in full accord with legislation. In the presence of papal protection and repression, medieval Jews suffered grotesque popular accusations and consequent mob violence, hardly to be restrained in the circumstances of medieval police powers. Crusaders rampaged through Jewish quarters on their way to the holy land; calumnies circulated that accused Jews of killing Christian children for ritual purposes; the appearance of the plague was a signal for accusations of well-poisoning. There is no evidence of papal reaction to Crusade pogroms that would match the efforts by Saint Bernard of Clairvaux to protect the Rhineland Jews.[21] The medieval "blood libel," however, drew the attention of an eighteenth century cardinal, himself to succeed to the papacy under the name Clement XIV (1769–1774). As Cardinal Ganganelli he assembled a dossier on the libel of ritual murder and its crucial documents, letters of Pope Innocent IV (1243–1254); this dossier has been given a definitive modern edition by the late Cecil Roth under the title *The Ritual Murder Libel and the Jew: The Report by Cardinal*

Lorenzo Ganganelli (*Pope Clement XIV*).[22] Needless to say, this edition by a distinguished modern Jewish historian constitutes in itself a guarantee of papal sincerity in the continuing effort to restrain anti-Jewish zealots and their libelous assaults against ancient Israel.

When the black death struck Europe, mobs ascribed it to well-poisoning by Jews and, too often proffered the option of baptism or death for the "crime." Pope Clement VI renewed the usual prohibitions of forced baptism on July 4, 1348, and on September 26 of the same year termed the accusation that Jews were responsible for the disastrous plague an "infamy" and pilloried the logic that would make Jews responsible for a pestilence "all but universal everywhere" afflicting "both Jews and many other nations to whom life in common with Jews is unknown." The accusation, therefore, in the pope's words "has no plausibility."[23]

Defenders of papal policies must regret the approval of Talmud burnings by popes who bowed to local pressures and, perhaps, were misled on the nature of that collection of Jewish traditional wisdom. Popes Gregory IX (1227–1241)[24] and Innocent IV (1243–1254) both ordered Talmuds to be burned, the second noting that the "immense book, exceeding the text of the Bible in size," containing as he had been assured "blasphemies against God and His Christ, and against the blessed Virgin . . . totally alien to the teaching of the Law. . . ."[25] Pope John XXII (1316–1334) defended Jews against the so-called "Pastorelli," a lawless populist pseudo-crusade,[26] against the accusation that Jews had incited lepers to poison wells. We have no evidence of his reaction, but he protected converts to Christianity from Judaism against confiscation;[27] on the other hand, he renewed anti-Talmud laws and abetted the Inquisitors' attacks against Jewish books.[28]

After so many admirable popes, the least admirable of them all, the notorious Alexander VI (1492–1503) showed the customary combination of positive and negative elements in his dealing with the Jews. On the negative side, the pope endorsed the degrading foot race that had to be run by Jews during Carnival.[29] On the positive side the same pope compelled recalcitrant Jewish communities within his civil jurisdiction to accept the fugitives from Spain of 1492;[30] so, too, his assignment of a Crusade tax on the clergy at the rate of a tenth of their income, whereas the tax he assigned to Jews was but a twentieth of theirs.[31] Like many a pope before him, Alexander VI employed a Jewish personal physician.[32]

More than twenty years ago materials such as these seemed to me worth organizing into a modest book. Rightly or wrongly my judgment was to give priority to persons rather than to their institutions; hence the title, *The Popes and the Jews in the Middle Ages.*[33] "Popes" and "Jews" are universal terms to be sure, but less abstract than "papacy" and "Judaism." Yet the most doctrinaire personalist must concede that persons act in and through the institutions they or their forebears have constructed; persons are finite, both in themselves and in the circumstances within which human options are made. Institutions are realities, "collaborators" it may be said, in the dialectic with those more active partners, human individuals.

In any case, my choice was to name popes and Jews, not papacy and Judaism.

PROFESSOR CUTLER'S CRITERIA

A friendly Jewish critic, Dr. Allan Harris Cutler, set out in a review his desiderata for such a study; he has lately restated the same criteria.[34] A rapid summary of his points will serve to indicate some of the complexities which bedevil the project of recovering our Jewish-Christian past. Dr. Cutler proposed, and proposes still, that to deal with medieval popes in this context demands (1) attention to each pope's total personality, biography, lifetime bibliography, his total program for the church, for the state, for western Christian society in general and, in that formidable context, his specific "Jewish policy;" (2) attention to the views of modern Catholic and Jewish scholars with respect to each pope, that study buttressed by attention to the views of Jews and Catholics who were contemporaries of those popes; (3) although historical study ought to be confined to "what happened and why," if evaluation be inescapable, the "highest possible ethical standards," as well as the standards prevalent in each pope's day, must be applied; (4) again, if evaluation must be made, then parallels ought to be drawn between each pope's Jewish policy and his policy toward heresies among Christians and toward Islam, as well as with contemporary rabbinic policies on relevant issues; (5) still under the same compulsion to judge, the "motives and results" of various policies, "not merely the policy itself" merits evaluation by the historian; (6) each pope's Jewish policies ought to be juxtaposed with what "the most recent research" discloses concerning his policies toward other non-Catholic groups, above all toward Muslims. These criteria, Dr. Cutler concedes, are "highly idealistic";[35] it is easy to agree. At the very least, the stance of the individual has been given unequivocal priority, since no mention has been made in the six criteria of a single institution.

PROFESSOR COHEN AND THE FRIARS

Professor Jeremy Cohen has emphasized in a recent book the fundamental role of institutions in shaping the response of even the most
dynamic popes to the Jews. He has, however, not failed to notice the
role of individuals and has devoted a series of chapters to Pablo Christiani and Raymond Martini of "the school of Raymond de Penaforte," to
Nicholas of Lyra and to Raymond Lull.[36] Despite these individuals to
whom he grants full value as effective agents of a deteriorating papal
policy, Professor Cohen has argued with great persuasiveness that the
new mendicant orders, Franciscans and Dominicans, introduced a new
dimension in the relationship between the papacy and Judaism. This is
not the place to engage in a review of this stimulating volume. My
reflections here arise from the materials there presented as seen from
the perspective of a methodological option between emphasis on individuals and emphasis on institutions. Dominicans and Franciscans,
teams of trained and dedicated religious, founded in reaction to threats
against the institutional church, were concerned above all with the unity
to which Christendom aspired. The presence of non-Christians within
Christian frontiers was seen as a challenge on both the theoretical and
on the practical plane. How ought the church and the papacy respond in
practice? How could that response be justified theologically? The Jews,
unlike Christian heretics, Muslems or Mongols, were seen to be involved ineluctably in the self-definition of the church. Jewish in her
founder, in her first archetypal decades, in her scriptures (only one
author of the specifically Christian scriptures was a Gentile), guided
consciously by the Hebrew prophets, her prayer life dominated by the
psalms, had there been no Jews, the church could not have come to be.
The relationship was seen as no accident of history, but as a clear dispensation of the Holy One. Alas, the theological explication of this family
bond had reached the Middle Ages in a most imperfect form; indeed, it
would be a daring modern theologian who would wish to claim that all is
clear today.[37] Theologically inspired difficulties brought forth on the
popular level an evil fruit of prejudice; uneasiness with "the other"
slipped over easily into resentment, fear, and hatred.

The other great source for the theologizing mendicants of the thirteenth century was the Greek philosophical tradition. For all the explicit
Aristotelianism of the period, this was profoundly in the tradition of
Plato and Plotinus, above all in its concern to make of The One both
source and end of all that is. Did this insight not coincide with the

biblical perception that the Lord is One (Dt 6:4) and that the One Lord of all is the sole end of all our striving—is this not also justified both by philosophy and by faith?

THE HUMAN GROUND OF PROFESSOR LANGMUIR

In addition to an emphasis on institutions and to exigent standards on individual popes, a third proposal has lately been added to the counsels of historians in search of an appropriate methodology. Professor Gavin Langmuir has commented on a pair of presentations by Jeremy Cohen and David Berger with his customary perceptiveness.[38] Beneath the ideological confrontation of Judaism and Christianity lie the causes which beget those "rationalizations."[39] He implies that historians of religious conflict fail to avail themselves of the sources normally canvassed in secular history, the springs of action rooted, not in what the religion of the human beings involved may be, but in the human as such.[40]

The very existence of this variety in approach to our common problem seems to indicate that the issue is one of emphasis. We are not in the presence of an exclusive disjunction, a clean-cut "either-or," one option of which is correct, the other incorrect. The third way, proposed by Professor Langmuir, can and must be subsumed within a balanced picture of the medieval encounter of Jews and Christians. He has rightly held that the Jew and the Christian are human—a scholastic would say they are human first "in the order of nature" and only at a non-chronologically "later" moment are they Christian or Jew. The fundamental human fact is that, for all our freedom—and it is real—we spontaneously institutionalize whatever we count as important. The obverse of that fact is that there is no institution which is not profoundly human in its genesis. This entails, among other things, that an institution need not preclude free action under its scope. Indeed, there are exercises of freedom that are inconceivable apart from institutionalization. Let the rules of chess be as rigid as you like; within them a chess master is free to choose among a number of opening moves, to mask his strategy, to deceive and surprise an opponent. That a knight does not move as a pawn does in no way precludes the freedom of the players; on the contrary, it proffers a freedom that a skilled player will know how to use to good purpose.

This is not to suggest that historians need not be circumspect in their weighing the roles of free individuals and of tightly structured institutions in the unpredictable drama which is human history.

1007 ANONYMOUS AND PROFESSOR STOW

To introduce yet another current volume without pretending to review it here (I have done so elsewhere in a brief way), Professor Kenneth Stow has produced a most remarkable study of a text, the "1007 Anonymous." Stow's opening lines advert to precisely our distinction between individual and institution; in doing so he adds another useful observation:

> There are three basic opinions on the subject of papal Jewish relations in the Middle Ages. . . . All three opinions, however, are unanimous in judging the Jewry policy of both the papacy as an institution and individual popes as well on the basis of the single issue of protection— or, as it is sometimes expressed, the favorable or unfavorable attitude adopted toward the Jews.[41]

Professor Stow has been right, it seems to me,[42] to put into relief the unfortunate restriction of our dialogue to the single question: Were the popes protective of Jews or the opposite in the Middle Ages?

A striking interpretation of "1007 Anonymous" here proposes that in fact the document is a veiled, thirteenth-century exhortation by a Jew to fellow Jews that they seek protection in time of trouble, not from secular princes, but from the pope. The unknown author was persuaded that a Jewish community under persecution could count on a consistent papal policy—an "institutionalized" tradition—whereas the favor of secular princes was unpredictable, laced with dangers that included expulsions, confiscations, even executions. That the author of the "Anonymous" recognized a consistent "papacy," instantiated successively in each pope, is clear from the fact that the pope of the document is nowhere named and historians, almost without exception, have glibly identified the named Christian figures and the events discussed with known eleventh-century persons and episodes.[43] Yet it is on the basis of institution that Professor Stow has controverted this popular wisdom. The document shows clear affinity with specifically thirteenth-century cultural developments, notably the "transvaluation" of the emerging nation-state into an ambiguous spiritual-temporal construct.[44] Indeed, the reservations conveyed to restrict an unhesitant turn to the papacy for protection was that papal power did not quite jibe with the extreme papal theory which "1007 Anonymous" explicitly favored. It may be noted that the passage cited to establish this echoes the celebrated formula of Pope Innocent III (1198–1216) on the place of a pope: "this side of God, but beyond man," *citra deum, sed ultra hominem.*[45] The document addressed an unnamed pope in these words:

> I have found none, save God, who stands above you as a ruler in the lands of the Nations. . . . I came to cry out about my ills *from the Jews who live under your jurisdiction.* . . .[46]

Since, in Jewish understanding, "the Nations" and "the Jews" constitute an exhaustive census of all races, the formula is equivalent to Innocent's *hominem,* that is, "the human" or, in the sense of a natural species, "man." Professor Stow (who has not made mention of this) notes that a papal claim to jurisdiction over Jews in religious matters appears explicitly for the first time in "the *Apparatus* to the *Decretals*" of Innocent IV (1243–1254) and argues that the conceptual scheme underlying the document is that of "mid-thirteenth century papal thought."[47] All of this is preliminary to the conclusions drawn by Professor Stow as to the ultimate significance of the document. Here we may legitimately call his presentation to the bar for the sake of its testimony to the dialectic of individual and institution; above all, of particular popes and the institution which is the papacy as crucial elements in the history of medieval Jews and Judaism. The rigorous criteria of Dr. Cutler have been adduced to illustrate one focus of the dialectic between universal and singular, individual and institution, that puzzled medieval schoolmen under the rubric of "the universal."

What is the promised analysis that tends to show persons and institutions in a fundamental harmony rather than in a disheartening disjunction?

Since Dr. Cutler noted that my primary academic concern has been with "medieval philosophy and logic,"[48] perhaps it will not be intolerable if some reflections of my own be set out on how popes and Jews, papacy and synagogue, persistent policy and transitory crises, seem to have begotten the historical realities we now seek to understand. In my philosophical youth "existentialist" philosophy wore the mantle of exciting novelty; for the existentialist of the strict observance there were no natures, no essences, nothing universal; human freedom made us all "creators" of meaning and value. During the sixties, youth in revolt warned all under thirty against trust in "institutions." What can be said in this year of grace concerning the institutions through which medieval individuals acted and were acted upon?

Surely a first reflection must be that institutions are contrived by human persons for human purposes and this with suspicious spontaneity. We have only to think of children playing: they establish new games with elaborate rules which they accept with joy and enforce with rigor. With maximum freedom the youngest among us willingly bind themselves by laws of their own making. Fashion in clothing tells a comparable story on the adult and, especially, on the adolescent level. In technologically simple societies as well as in the most "developed" cultures, clothing never remains on the utilitarian plane of warmth and protection. What we wear is "institutionalized." Clothes become a kind of language; striped trousers say one thing, blue jeans another. What blue jeans say can be heard around the globe; jeans have become a uniform, freely adopted by precisely those who are the least inclined to accept traditional practices. It is remarkable that what is worn announces the police, the surgeon, the rabbi, the soldier, the conservative. Clothes can say "I am a bride" or "I am in mourning." To wear a hat in a given setting or, under other circumstances, to remove it, expresses respect or outrages sensibilities. As Marshal McLuhan used to say, "We have no clothes, only costumes."

Like games and clothing, "the papacy" is an institutionalization by a long line of creative popes. Their action has been "creative" in that it could not have been predicted, was not implicit in their points of departure. It is a paradoxical fact, for instance, that the notion of papal infallibility was strongly resisted by many a medieval pope who saw it as a limitation of his own freedom of action by the dead hands of predecessors. As all historians know, the ascription of a carefully circumscribed "infallibility" to certain papal pronouncements was a nineteenth century, not a medieval, development. Still, despite distrust of "infallibility" medieval popes honored many facets of the jurisprudence inherited from pagan Rome, among them a tendency to the practice of *stare decisis:* "to stand by decisions that had been taken." This gave impressive continuity to the policies of popes through the centuries, and nowhere is this more evident than in the Jewish policy of the medieval papacy. Think, for instance, of the papal constitution called from its opening words *Sicut Iudaeis non.* This elaborate document seems to have grown by steady accretion from a single phrase in a policy letter of Pope Gregory I (590–604).[49] Somewhat as the phrase "wall of separation" (between church and state) in a private letter from Thomas Jefferson to a clergyman has become the nucleus of constitutional discourse in the United States, so Pope Gregory's formula served as the core around which a full-fledged papal-Jewish policy developed. Thus it has been that the Petrine office, as Roman Catholics think of the papacy, is in human terms an institutionalization of what pope after pope received and transmitted. Developments were occasioned by papal response to crises that arose during each pope's tenure of the office. True enough, Catholics are persuaded that the Spirit is at work in all ecclesial experience, not least in the papacy, but beneath and within grace, as they see it, lies nature: institutionalization is natural to our race.

Let us conclude with the borrowed terms with which we began. From the scholar we have the right to demand erudition, percipience, judgment, and balance. From the saint one expects a passion for truth at all costs, charity no matter what sacrifice this may entail. If you say that this is no more than what a scholar must provide, then to that point to be a scholar is to be something of a saint. Even scholastics have their widow's mite to contribute. They were, and are, strong on clear definition, strong on the basic sequence so well formulated by Aristotle that "certain things being stated, something other than what is stated follows of necessity from their being so" (*Prior Analytics* 1, 1; 24b 19–21). Scholastics live and move and have their being in just this ambience, but they have not willingly remained on the constricted plane of the single syllogism. A perilous thirst for all-encompassing systems has often betrayed scholastics into premature explanations and programs. No century was more fruitfully "scholastic" than was the thirteenth. Often enough, and Professor Cohen has seen the phenomenon clearly, the manipulation of abstractions tempted mendicant theologians and canonists into woefully inadequate conceptual schemes, intellectual failures in the first instance, but failures that papal power turned into disasters for the Jews. It is hard to be just to an abstraction and impossible to be a friend to abstract Judaism. Yet many a medieval pope could have a Jewish friend, entrust his health to a Jewish physician (with suitable dispensation from his own law), legislate for justice to the Jews. Still, this is hardly the whole story. "1007 Anonymous" bears witness that one Jewish author saw in the institutional papacy—made up of individuals as human as any king, but predictable and reliable because their decisions coalesced into a policy—for all its limitations, consistent and perennial.

NOTES

* Dr Jaroslav Pelikan, Lecture 5: "Scholastics, Scholars, and Saints."

1. "Gelasius Quinigesio episcopo: Vir clarissimus Telesinus, quamvis Judaicae credulitatis videatur, talem se nobis approbare contendit, ut merito nostrum

appellare debeamus; qui pro Antonio parente suo specialiter postulavit ut eum dilectioni tuae commendare debeamus; et ideo fratrem supradictum voluntatis nostrae mandatorumque respectu ita se habere convenit ut non solum in nullo penitus opprimatur, verum etiam in quo ei opus fuerit tuae se gaudeat dilectione adjutum." PL 59 146 C. (PL= J.P. Migne, *Patrologiae cursus . . . series latina*).

2. ". . . Quapropter diligenter vestra inter utrumque sollicitudo rerum fideliter examinet veritatem, quatenus nec religio temerata videatur, nec servus hac obsectione mentitus competentis jura domini declinare contendat." PL 59 146 D–147 A.

3. ". . . sicut legalis definitio Iudaeos novas non patitur erigere synagogas, ita quoque eos sine inquietudine veteres habere permittit." MGH, Epistolarum Lib. IX, 195, vol. II, pp.182–184. (MGH= *Monumenta Germaniae historica*).

4. Ibid., "Ne ergo suprascriptus Petrus vel alii qui ei in hac indisciplinationis pravitate praebuere solacium sive consensum hoc zelo fidei se fecisse respondeant . . . scire debent, quia haec circa eos temperantia magis utenda est, ut trahatur ab eis velle, non ut ducantur inviti. . . ."

5. "Sicut Iudaeos non debet esse licentia quicquam in synagogis suis ultra quam permissum est lege praesumere, ita in his quae eis concessa sunt nullum debent praeiudicium sustinere. . . ." Ibid. VIII, 25, vol. II, p. 27.

6. Ibid. II, 38, vol. I, pp. 133–139 and V, 7, vol. I, pp. 288–289.

7. ". . . multos consistentium in illis partibus Iudaeorum vi magis ad fontem baptismatis quam praedicatione perductos. . . . Adhibendus ergo illis est sermo . . . et eorum quantos Deus donaverit ac regenerationem novae vitae perducat." Ibid., I, 45, vol. I, pp. 71, 72.

8. Gratian, *Decretum* pars I, distinctio 45, canon 3, *Corpus iuris canonici,* ed. A.L. Richterus, A. Friedberg (Leipzig: 1879), vol. I, col. 160.

9. "Quid autem de episcopis, qui verberibus timeri volunt, canones dicant, bene fraternitas vestra novit. Pastores etenim facti sumus, non persecutores. . . . Nova vero atque inaudita est ista praedicatio, quae verberibus exigit fidem." MGH, Epist. III, 52, vol. I, pp. 208, 209.

10. "Imo etsi Judaei cogi non possint ad suscipiendum Baptismum, tamen si de facto coacti illum suscipiant, adhuc sub poenis haereticorum resilire non possunt . . . dummodo tamen coactio non fuerit absoluta. . . . Si enim quis per vim non conditionatam, sed absolutam, Baptismum suscipiat, Christianus dici non potest, et consequenter uti talis ad Fidem servandam cogi nequit." V. Petra, *Commentaria ad apostolicas seu bullas singulas summorum pontificum* (Venice: 1741) vol. III, p. 256, no 6.

11. See *Prudentii Trecensis annales,* anno 839, MGH, Scriptorum I, 433, ll. 4–20.

12. "Bodo, qui ante annos aliquot Christiana veritate derelicta ad Judaeorum perfidiam concesserat, in tantum mali profecit, ut in omnes Christianos Hispaniae degentes, tam Regis quam gentis Sarracenorum animos concitare statuerit, quatenus aut relicta Christianae fidei Religione ad Judaeorum insaniam,

Sarracenorum dementiam se converterent, aut certe omnes interfice-rentur. . . ." *Anales Bertinianos,* anno 847 *España Sagrada,* vol. X, p. 578.

13. ". . . monemus, ut in terra tua Judaeos christianis dominari vel supra eos potestatem exercere ulterius nullatenus sinas." MGH Epistolarum selectarum IX, vol. II, p. 571.

14. ". . . praecipimus Iudaeis dominis habere servos Christianos hac tumtaxat condicione permissa, ut propriam religionem eos servare permittant. . . ." *Codex Theodosiani* 16, 9, 3, *Theodosiani libri xvi. . .* ed. Th. Mommsen, P. Krueger (Berlin: 1922), vol. I, p. 896.

15. "Si quis Iudaeorum Christianum mancipium vel cuiuslibet alterius sectae mercatus circumciderit, minime in servitute retineat circumcisum, sed libertatis privilegiis, qui hoc sustinuerit, potiatur." Ibid., 16, 9, 1, vol. I, p. 895; also: ". . . mancipium fisco protinus vindicetur; si vero emptum circumciderit, non solum mancipii damno mulctetur, verum etiam capitali sententia puniatur . . . omnia, quae apud eum repperiuntur, protinus auferantur. . . ." Ibid. 16, 9, 2, vol. I, p. 896; variations in the law reflect Roman legal practice by which law originated in decrees of successive emperors.

16. ". . . Judaei a Christianis graves et immoderatas usuras extorserint . . ." Titulus LXVII IV Lateran Council, G.D. Mansi, *Sacrorum conciliorum nova et amplissima collectio* (Florence: 1759–1798), vol. XXII, coll. 1054–1058 for decisions cited. The same "Title" of the council decrees included legislation on tithes: "Ac eadem poena Judaeos decernimus compellandos ad satisfaciendum ecclesiis pro decimis et oblationibus debitis, quas a Christianis de domibus et possessionibus aliis percipere consueverant, antequam ad Judaeos quocumque titulo devenissent. . . ." Ibid.

17. "In nonnullis provinciis a Christianis Judaeos seu Saracenos habitus distinguit diversitas: sed in quibusdam sic quaedam inolevit confusio ut nulla differentia discernantur . . . statuimus ut . . . qualitate habitus publice ab aliis populis distinguantur. . . ." Titulus LXVII, ibidem.

18. ". . . ne Judaei officiis publicis praeferantur. . . ." Titulus LXIX, ibid.

19. "In diebus autem lamentationis, et Dominicae passionis, in publicum minime prodeant (Judaei), eo quod nonnulli ex ipsis, talibus diebus (sicut accepimus) ornatius non erubescunt incedere, ac Christianis, qui sacratissimae passionis memoriam exhibentes lamentationis signa praetendunt, illudere non formidant." Titulus LXVII, ibid.

20. See below, *The "1007 Anonymous" and Papal Sovereignty,* ed. K.R. Stow (Cincinnati; 1984).

21. Having preached the Second Crusade, Bernard of Clairvaux intervened effectively against disorders to which the Crusaders had been aroused by the preaching of a zealot monk named Rudolph and managed to persuade Rudolph to return to his monastery.

22. This title, published in London, carries no date of publication; its modern edition by a Jewish scholar of Roth's stature guarantees its significance on this

aspect of papal attitudes in the presence of the worst medieval calumny against the Jews.

23. "Nuper ad nostrum fama publica, seu infamia verius, perduxit auditum, quod nonnulli Christiani pestem, qua Deus populum Christianum ipsius peccatis populi provocatus affligit, Judaeorum falso tossicationibus seducente diabolo imputantes . . . per diversa mundi climata Judaeos ipsos ac alias natione plurimas, quae cohabitationem Judaeorum eorumdem non noverant, pestis haec ubique fere communis affixit occulto Dei judicio et affligit; proinde verisimilitudo non recipit, quod Judaei praedicti occasionem tanto flagitio praestiterint sive causam. . . ." For the text of this letter, see Baronius-Raynaldus, *Annales ecclesiastici* vol. XXV, 455, no. 33.

24. *Anonymus Erfordiensis:* "Circa festum S. Michaelis, (29 September) rex Franciae propter nimiam studii sui . . . XXIII carractas librorum suorum (Judaeorum) Parisiis incendio jussit cremari." Baronius-Raynaldus, vol. XXI, 285, note 1.

25. See Baronius-Raynaldus, vol. XXI, 285, no. 41 for text of this letter which is only calendared in Innocent's *Les registres* . . . vol. I, 115, no 682.

26. Baronius-Raynaldus, vol. XXIV, 128, no. 24 and 127, no. 22.

27. See Pope John's *Lettres secrètes et curiales,* vol. I, cols. 938, 939 as well as his *Extravagantes communes* V, 2, 2; *Corpus iuris canonici,* vol. II, col. 1290.

28. See *Vitae paparum Avenionensium,* ed. E. Baluze (Paris: 1914–1927), vol. III, 243, also Baronius-Raynaldus, vol. XXIV, 128–131, nos. 24–30.

29. "Martis, XVII februarii et sequentibus diebus, Judei et ceteri cucurrerunt pro palliis, more solito, et alia festa bestialia romana habita solemniter." *Rerum Italicarum scriptores,* XXXII, 1, vol. II, p. 224.

30. ". . . ipsique Judei, si christianis pressura obvenerit, quod Deus pro sua clementia avertat, detrimentum essent participes et eorum periculo uti nostro res ageretur." Ibid.

31. Ibid., p. 226.

32. Notably, Maestro Boneto (or Bonet de Lattes, Bonet Provenziali) who had come to Rome via the papal city of Carpentras in Provence.

33. New York: 1965.

34. Review in *The Journal of Ecumenical Studies* 5.1 (Winter, 1968) 153–155; see also, A.H. Cutler and H.E. Cutler, *The Jew as Ally of the Muslim: Medieval Roots of Anti-Semitism* (Note Dame: 1986), pp. 15–21.

35. Review cited, p. 154; *The Jew as Ally,* p. 18.

36. J. Cohen, *The Friars and the Jews: The Evolution of Medieval Anti-Judaism* (Ithaca and London, 1982); reference is to chapters 5 through 8.

37. "Today, as a matter of fact, perhaps in contrast to patristic and medieval theology, we do not have a clear, reflective theology of this break, this new beginning of Christianity with Paul as its inaugurator (i.e., the events recorded in Acts 15); perhaps that will only gradually be worked out in a dialogue with the Synagogue of today." K. Rahner, "Toward a Fundamental Theological Interpre-

tation of Vatican II," *Theological Studies* 40 (1979) p. 723; for the German text, see *Schriften zur Theologie*, Bd XIV, Zurich, 1980, S. 296.

38. See *The American Historical Review*, 91.3 (June 1986), AHR Forum: "Mission to the Jews and Jewish-Christian Contacts in the Polemical Literature of the High Middle Ages," D. Berger, pp. 576–591; "Scholarship and Intolerance in the Medieval Academy: The Study and Evaluation of Judaism in European Christendom," J. Cohen, pp. 592–613; "Comment," G.J. Langmuir, pp. 614–624.

39. See "Comment," p. 615.

40. Ibid.

41. K. R. Stow, *The "1007 Anonymous" and Papal Sovereignty: Jewish Perceptions of the Papacy and Papal Policy in the High Middle Ages* (Cincinnati: 1984), p. 1.

42. "Whether it was a benign or a tyrannical dispensation that put popes in a position to exercise politically supported power over the Jews is a part of the infinitely broader question of the two Cities men construct for time and for eternity. The vestiges of the Jewish-papal encounter must be taken into account if the larger question is to be weighed, but it is not to be hoped that the whole might be discovered within this part. . . ." *The Popes and the Jews in the Middle Ages*, p. 164.

43. Stow, op. cit. p. 27; see also p. 57, note 111.

44. Ibid., pp. 33 ff.

45. *Sermo II in consecratione pontificis maximi*, PL 217 658 A.

46. Stow, op. cit. pp. 35, 36.

47. Ibid., p. 37

48. Review cited above, note 34, p. 155; *The Jew as Ally*, p. 19.

49. *The Popes and the Jews*, pp. 35–47; for an English translation of a developed form of this document, see Appendix VI, pp. 230–232.

IV.
JUDAISM AND CHRISTIANITY
ENTER THE MODERN WORLD

The Reformation and the Jews

Alice L. Eckardt

The Reformation is often presented as the beginning of the modern world, but I would argue that the Reformation, at least in its sixteenth-century form, is not really modern in its basic conceptions or intentions. The preceding century of Renaissance was much more modern with its interest in pre-Christian literature, philosophy, and culture, its readiness to engage in objective and scientific study (even of some sacrosanct documents), its greater openness to the erudition of Muslim and Jewish scholars, and its somewhat more generally secular outlook. In fact, the Reformation was to a considerable degree a reaction against the Renaissance, an attempt to reassert the vitality of a total Christian civilization, such as medieval Christendom represented, but purified by the removal of irrelevant or false ecclesiastical and doctrinal accretions that stood in the way of a proper understanding of God's action in Christ and the redemption of the world which that event was intended to accomplish.

Only in a very few figures of the magisterial Reformation, and in some aspects of the left-wing Reformation, do we find even beginning possibilities of a new understanding of Judaism and a new relationship to the Jewish people. By and large the reformers continued the church's *adversus Judaeos* tradition, some more vehemently than others, even in the new circumstances of the breakup of the papal-dominated church and the emergence of new national and independent churches. These conditions generally did not improve the Jewish situation and in most cases worsened it. The polemics of the verbal warfare between Catholics and Protestants, between Lutherans and Calvinists, between mainline Protestants and sectarians and those called heretics caught Jews in the

111

crossfire just as military battles usually did. No accusation was seen as more condemning of one's opponent than that of "Judaizer."

We must recognize that toleration was a rare commodity in the sixteenth century; it was not considered to be a virtue since false belief and teaching were held responsible for destroying souls and bringing God's vengeance on all involved parties.[1] The ideal, rather, was monolithic Christian unity. The breakup of this monolith put an end to Jews being the only religious minority.

In this period Jewish views also remained primarily traditional, with the conviction that Judaism represented the purest form of faith and the way of life most closely attuned to the divine will. Both sides—Christian and Jewish—looked and hoped for the conversion of the other to its own truth. Thus, new movements within either community were evaluated in terms of this possible outcome, or the reverse—a hardening of positions and antagonism.

Nevertheless, *in the long run* the Reformation did unleash forces of change that had much to do with bringing the modern world into existence—with, to be sure, the negative developments of narrowly nationalistic societies and modern antisemitism as well as the positive developments of religious liberty and pluralism.

The reformers of the first stage are dominated by the figure of Martin Luther. He was a figure of compelling conviction and invincible power; an advocate who could become a raging opponent; a man who recognized and utilized the potency of the printed word, who used coarse and brutal language against any and all antagonists and yet produced a magnificent German translation of the Bible that shaped the modern German language and literary style; a person who appealed to nationalist aspirations of princes and people but advised ruthless suppression of the revolt of the oppressed peasantry rather than have his reform be seen as a social revolution.

Luther set out to reform the one church and the Christian state within the framework of the medieval synthesis. He saw scripture as the only genuine source of truth and therefore was concerned with its interpretation in the church's theology and structure since the church was meant to be the people of God by virtue of faith alone. An institutional church that focused on rituals and priestly roles made salvation into a mechanical process and therefore utterly useless: "Because the Papists, *like the Jews,* insist that anyone wishing to be saved must observe their ceremonies, they will perish *like the Jews.*"[2] There was no truth outside the gospel. Luther was not open to other points of view; he was absolutely certain that he had received doctrine "from heaven and by the grace of God,"[3] and a mission to deliver it. Since there was only one truth and only one way of salvation, Luther came to be just as committed to rooting out heresy as the patristic and medieval church had been. Heretics were tools of the devil who led the gullible faithful into sin and eternal damnation. When the historical situation led him to turn to the princes, as the civil arm of Christendom, since the clergy, the sacerdotal arm of Christendom, had failed to correct abuses in the church, and when his reformed church became the established state church, the question of religious belief became further complicated by the issue of civic loyalty or treason. Moreover, Luther himself became less and less willing to allow other forms of Christianity a public role: the mass was forbidden as "blasphemy" by 1525, and the proper state authority was expected to suppress it; as of 1529 people were to be forced to attend the sermon even if they did not believe, so that they would learn at least the "outward works of obedience"; and in 1531 he agreed that Anabaptists and other Protestant extremists could be "done to death by the civil authority."[4]

But these measures were directed at other Christians; what about Jews? Although Luther was quite prepared to make radical changes in the proclamation of the gospel (to make it rest on faith alone) and in church practices and government (to remove mechanical representation of redemption, end clerical celibacy, and abolish all "Judaic" emphasis on works-righteousness), he saw no need to alter the *adversus Judaeos* tradition of Christian teaching. Anti-Judaism was so embedded in Christianity by this time that practically no one in the church could imagine removing it without thereby disavowing the gospel. In Luther's first writing on the Jews, in 1514–1515 (before his initial challenge to Rome), he reiterated the traditional church position that God had rejected the Jewish people. Their situation of insecurity and dispersal throughout the world made this obvious to anyone not blinded by willful obstinacy. Yet Jews had not learned from this divine punishment, and they remained obdurate foes of Christianity (hence of God), wishing to lead others astray also. Only a small remnant of them would be saved according to his interpretation of Old Testament prophesies.

Does Luther's well-known writing of 1521, *That Jesus Christ Was Born a Jew,* indicate that he broke with this traditional anti-Judaism? His language is temperate (for him) and his strategy is humane: Christians are to be guided "by the law of Christian love" in dealing with Jews, should receive them cordially, and permit them to work and trade with

Christians. He argued that treating Jews with scorn and arrogance, and making false accusations against them was hardly going to attract them: "If the apostles, who also were Jews, had dealt with us Gentiles as we Gentiles deal with the Jews, there would never have been a Christian among the Gentiles. . . . we in our turn ought to treat the Jews in a brotherly manner. . . ." He admitted that "after all, we ourselves are not all good Christians either." He noted that God has not granted to any other nation "so high an honor as he has to the Jews. For from among the Gentiles there have been raised up no patriarchs, no apostles, no prophets, indeed, very few genuine Christians either. . . . He committed the Holy Scriptures, that is, the law and the prophets [to no others]." Nevertheless, the main thrust of the second half of the treatise was an "elaborate argument from Scripture and history to convince the Jews of Christ's messiahship," along with a plea to fellow Christians to treat Jews more kindly in the hope of converting "some of them." Luther did not expect a mass conversion. He closed by saying, "Here I will let the matter rest for the present, until I see what I have accomplished."[5]

Martin Luther was, in fact, using much the same argumentation utilized over centuries when Christians tried to persuade Jews that the Old Testament points forward to Christ, and that the New Testament testimony is reliable as well as consistent with earlier prophecies.[6] Even Luther's recommendation of kindness as an instrument of conversion was commensurate with much papal policy. In other words, he had not broken with the past for all his legitimate denunciation of "the papists" on this score. Heiko Oberman points out that "Luther's critique of Judaism is just as uncompromising in 1523 [even if more mildly expressed] as it is in the later years: Christianity and Judaism are mutually exclusive; Reformation does not imply salvation for Jews." "The basis of Luther's anti-Judaism was the conviction that ever since Christ's appearance on earth, the Jews have had no more future as Jews."[7]

Although Luther did not make any practical attempts to alleviate the Jews' situation in Saxony or elsewhere, his admonition regarding kind treatment apparently had some prompt effect among his followers, according to Rabbi Abraham b. R. Eliezer Halevi writing at the time.[8] Unfortunately, this was not to endure for very long. None of the reformers protested when the emperor imposed the yellow badge on all Jews in his domain. When in August, 1536 the Elector John Frederick ordered all Jews to leave Saxony (perhaps even on Luther's advice[9]), Rabbi Josel of Rosheim approached Luther with a letter of introduction and an appeal from a fellow reformer of Strasbourg, Wolfgang Capito, for him to intercede on behalf of the Jews. Capito used a form of Luther's own 1523 position in arguing that the Jews should be helped so that they would realize that Christians "are prepared to treat kindly . . . even our enemies."[10] But Luther refused to intercede because he was certain that such action would only increase Jewish obstinacy, and that nothing but acceptance of their "kinsman and Lord, the beloved crucified Jesus Christ" could "reverse the misery of the Jewish exile."[11]

In 1543 (twenty years after writing *That Jesus Christ Was Born a Jew*) Luther produced three works dealing specifically with Jews: *On the Last Words of David; Von Schem Hamphoras* ("Concerning the Ineffable Name"), and *On the Jews and Their Lies*. Even if we were to ignore the first two because of their viciousness, hatred, lack of human decency, and incoherence,[12] we would need to recognize that they went beyond attacking Jews as persons and also dealt with Jewish sources in similar fashion. The last of the three (actually the first one written) attacked the Jews' false pride (of lineage and homeland), their "works-righteousness" (reliance on the covenant of circumcision and the law), their false interpretation of key biblical passages, their calumnies against Jesus and Mary, their hatred for *Goyim* and crimes against Christendom. (Here he specifically mentioned the accusations that they poison the wells, kidnap and pierce the children, and use the blood of Christians.[13]) All three of the 1543 writings were based on Luther's conviction that Jews had the "evil desire" to convert Christians: ". . . the Jews would like to entice us Christians to their faith and they do this whenever they can."[14]

The last section of *On the Jews and Their Lies* asks, "What shall we Christians do with this rejected and condemned people? Since they live among us, we dare not tolerate their conduct, now that we are aware of [it, because] if we do, we become sharers in their lies, cursing, and blasphemy . . . we cannot extinguish the . . . fire of divine wrath, . . . nor can we convert the Jews. [Therefore,] we must practice sharp mercy to see whether we might save at least a few from the glowing flames." Then followed his now well-known advice, which was not just given once but three times: burn their synagogues, schools, and houses, and bury all traces of them, remove all their prayer books and Talmudic writings, forbid their rabbis to teach, abolish safe-conduct for them on the highways, prohibit usury to them, and take away all cash and treasure of gold and silver.[15] (It is no wonder that Professor Jules Isaac, coming across these words in the midst of the *Shoah* and his people's and family's suffering, should write: "Patience, Luther, Hitler will come. Your wishes will be granted, and more! Let us recognize here the family ties, the blood ties, uniting two great Germans, and let us place Luther in the place he deserves, in the first row of Christian precursors . . . of Auschwitz."[16])

The last words (almost literally) of Martin Luther once again dealt with the Jews. As he traveled to Eisleben in January–February, 1546, plagued by a multitude of ills and pains,[17] he wrote to his wife that he "must do something about these Jews" still living in some villages, and about a Countess who was protecting a few of them.[18] At the end of his sermon, delivered but a few hours before he died, he spoke to the Eisleben congregation about the need to bring their Jewish neighbors to the baptismal font. But *if* such efforts should be unsuccessful, "*then* we must not suffer them to remain for they daily abuse and blaspheme Christ. . . . you must not be a partaker in the sins of others."[19]

In these last three years we find Luther advocating a very different policy from that of 1523, and a radical one on all counts. Why? The usual explanation that he was disillusioned and embittered by the Jews' failure to embrace Christianity after the reforms and more kindly treatment he advocated is inadequate. It does not pay sufficient attention to his earlier opposition and antipathy and the consistent anti-Jewish polemic in his biblical commentaries and lectures. Oberman offers an alternative: that Luther was an apocalyptic who was convinced that the Reformation was the beginning of the end of time, with three stages. The first was his own discovery and proclamation of the true gospel; the second, the organizing of the reform congregations through catechism, liturgical and institutional reform; and finally, the Counter-Reformation, by which he meant not only the Catholic Church's counterattack, but also the amassing of all the opposing forces of Antichrist and Devil against the true church: the Turks threatening Germany, "Sabbatarians" embracing the Jewish law, Anabaptists and other "false Christians" within the ranks of the Protestant church creating dissent and deserting the gospel. These signs indicated to him that the time left before the end must be very brief. Consequently, Luther had no more time for patience with the Jews. Their very presence might bring God's vengeance down on their hosts. So if even new harsh conditions would not bring them into the church, then they must be thrust out of the Protestants' realm.[20]

At the time a number of Luther's colleagues were somewhat disturbed and embarrassed by these particular writings. Heinrich Bullinger in Zurich denounced Luther's "lewd and houndish eloquence" and "scurrility," and considered *Vom Schem Hamphoras* to be "most vilely written." Andreas Osiander wrote to Elias Levita expressing his severe disapprobation, and also criticizing a number of Luther's inaccuracies. Philip Melanchthon, the devoted disciple but also a seeker after harmony among the various reformers, kept knowledge of Osiander's letter from Luther out of fear over the latter's reaction.[21] Fortunately none of the rulers of the time acted on Luther's advice, although when the emperor died, most of the German states expelled any remaining Jews.

What may be more interesting, however, is the apparent lack of popular response to these later writings; a much smaller number of them were purchased. Salo Baron believes the public was resentful of the uncouthness of these anti-Jewish tracts, even though they normally enjoyed the mutual recriminations of the theological opponents.[22] Could it be that there was so much of this type of literature available that it simply did not create the same interest as Luther's other writings, which had a spiritual force to them despite the invective that was so endemic? Or can we draw some kind of parallel between the popular responses to Luther's two stages of anti-Jewish writings and advice, and to Hitler's two stages: his virulent denunciations and early actions against Jews, and then the "Final Solution" when people came to know more precisely what that involved? With both Luther and Hitler people were quite ready to accept the generalized verbal attacks and the discriminatory legislation. But when the logic of negation and reprobation was carried forward to include, in Luther's case, wholesale destruction and confiscation of personal and community property, removal of public protection for persons, and the death sentence for teaching Judaism, and in Hitler's case, the desecration and destruction of all synagogues, and the indiscriminate murder of all Jews, a smaller proportion of the public apparently was ready to approve. Did a residue of humaneness, or a sense of certain limits to acceptable behavior, persist in both communities? Unfortunately, in each instance, previous boundaries were crossed, and ominous precedents created.

Because the Jews were at the center of Luther's theology in a number of ways, and because Luther's influence was and remained so extensive, a few more observations about him are necessary:

1. For him the Jews' refusal to accept Jesus as Messiah was a central point of holy scripture and of postbiblical history. They were a "terrifying witness" to the "state of sin and unbelief to which all [people] would be consigned save for God's mercy." Biblical prophecy of salvation is not addressed to Jews as Jews; therefore Christians may "despair" of them "with a clear conscience."[23]

2. They represented the human willfulness that seeks to manipulate and control God, through ceremonial law or a priest-controlled sacramental system that is essentially "Judaic" though found equally in the Roman church and even among "false Christians" within Protestantism. ("Many [Christian] Hebraists are more rabbinical than Christian."[24]) Luther never yielded; conversion was the only route of salvation for Jews (as reform was for Christians).

3. Luther used "works" almost interchangeably with the Jews and their law and he consistently harangued against it. "It [became] a code word for the enemy and nemesis that threatens true Christian salvation." Moreover, as Rabbi Sholom Singer has observed, "if the church lives in original sin, Jews live in double sin, that of sinning and causing others to sin, . . . more grievously misguiding others."[25]

4. His lifetime preoccupation with the Hebrew Bible (on which he spent two-thirds of his teaching years) made him less friendly, rather than more, to Jews of his day. Their stubborn adherence to their own interpretation of scripture infuriated him and convinced him that it was a result of Satan standing alongside them.[26]

5. The *hutzpah* of Jews attempting to convert Christians to Judaism (though the opposite was, of course, obligatory), and the "backward" step that some few Christian groups were taking in emulating such Jewish practices as circumcision and the seventh-day sabbath was responsible in part for the vitriolic nature of his later writings.

6. Although Luther used the same kind of extreme language toward all opponents as toward Jews, in the latter case he complemented his denunciations with practical proposals to German princes as to how they could make life more miserable for Jews.

7. There was violence, not just in Luther's language but, more important, in his theology. His "ideological Messianism" left no place, no dignity, no rights to those who would not accept it: "Whoever does not accept and honor [the New Testament] does not accept and honor God the Father himself."[27]

8. Luther was inconsistent (along with most Christian tradition) with regard to the theological interpretation of suffering. When Christians suffered, it was a sign that they were God's new Israel, sharing in the suffering of Christ and as martyrs to the truth of the gospel. But when Jews experienced suffering, it was a sign of God's rejection and punishment of them for their iniquities.

9. Luther was convinced that Jewish homelessness was such an overwhelming proof of God's rejection that he took an oath: "If it should

happen that the diaspora comes to an end, and Jews are led back to Jerusalem, then we Christians will follow on their heels and ourselves 'become Jews.' " Luther continued: "Or if such an event fails to come about, then let them head for Jerusalem, build temples, set up priesthoods, principalities, Moses with his laws, and in other words themselves become Jews again and take the land into their possession. For when this happens, they will see us come quickly on their heels and likewise become Jews. But if not, then it is entirely ludicrous that they would want to persuade us into accepting their degenerate laws, which are surely by now after fifteen hundred years of decay no longer laws at all. And should we believe what they themselves do not and cannot believe, as long as they do not have Jerusalem and the land of Israel?"[28]

One other Lutheran leader of the time deserves mention—Justus Jonas. He emphasized the common features of Jews' and Christians' destinies: both had been led astray—Jews by Talmudic hair-splitting, Christians by scholastic subtleties. Christians would be won to the cause of reform by recovery of their holy scriptures, and Jews by "entrusting themselves to the unadulterated" *Tanakh* (that is, giving up the Talmud). Christians should recognize Jews as their brethren and companions in destiny, and therefore include them in their prayers. Christians are guests in the house of Abraham and are united in one body with Jews—under the single head of Jesus Christ. For that reason the church has a responsibility for the mission to the Jews to save as many as possible "from a sinking ship," and he considered Luther's *That Jesus Christ Was Born a Jew* an excellent missionary tract. When Jonas translated some of Luther's works into Latin, he deliberately modified some of the harshest words and arguments, even substituting some of his own ideas. Jonas believed it was more urgent to convert the heathen than the Jews.[29] Jonas's ideas were certainly unprecedented and un-Lutheran. But unfortunately he did not have the impact Luther did.

When we consider the Calvinist or Reformed tradition, we find that Ulrich Zwingli, who led Zurich into the Reformation camp, censured the Catholic Church for its "judaizing ceremonies," but he had very little consciousness of contemporary Jewry. He followed a more or less traditional theology that saw Jews as once having been God's people, but no longer, having been replaced by Gentile Christians. "There is only one people of God, not two." He held a fairly liberal doctrine of election that saw righteous non-Christians as included in that election, although *no postbiblical Jews* were listed among some ancient Greeks, Romans, and biblical figures.[30]

Heinrich Bullinger, who following Zwingli in the main Zurich pulpit, insisted more than any other reformer on the unity of the Old and New Testaments, though he held that Jews were wrong in refusing to interpret the Old in light of the New dispensation. However, he also insisted that despite all appearances, Jews still "possessed the divine promise and selection."[31] Unfortunately, neither Bullinger nor Zwingli fully developed these ideas that were positive toward Jews and Judaism.

With John Calvin we are faced with a complex amalgam of negative and positive positions. He was probably influenced during his two years of exile in Strasbourg by Martin Bucer's traditionally harsh views toward Jews rather than by Capito's relatively greater tolerance. Bucer accused Jews of raging and blaspheming against "our Lord," hating and persecuting Christians, leading a "decadent, selfish and idle life," and corrupting Christians (through bribes) to defend them. Moreover, he advised the ruler of Hesse to require Jews to do "the most despicable, burdensome, and unpleasant jobs" including breaking stone, making charcoal, cleaning out chimneys and latrines.[32]

But we find the same ambivalence in Bucer as we find in so many other churchmen and reformers. For example, commenting on Paul's letter to the church at Rome, he wrote, "we must oppose and love [the Jews] at the same time, and treat them as both enemies and friends— enemies because of their infidelity and for the sake of the saints among the Gentiles, to whom the Jews stubbornly denied participation in the Kingdom of God" and "friends because of their original selection as God's people and for the sake of the Patriarchs, whose physical descendants they indubitably are." Bucer took a strong conversionist position: "We must view this people even now as one which must be preserved and maintained until its ultimate salvation." Yet he was suspicious of those very converts.[33]

Bucer and his colleague Wolfgang Capito lived in relatively close proximity to Jewish communities near Strasbourg that had relatively good relations with their Christian neighbors at that time. By contrast, Calvin and the other Swiss reformers had no immediate contact with Jews because the Swiss cantons had expelled them in the fifteenth century and made no move to readmit them in the sixteenth.[34]

With regard to the Mosaic law, John Calvin took a very positive stand; it is, he said, a teaching of perfect righteousness. It is embedded in every person's conscience. But God also wrote it down because we cannot tolerate "inward accusation." If anyone *entirely and exactly* fulfills all that is commanded, "he will be rewarded with eternal life." But if anyone fails to observe every detail of the law, "he will receive the condemnation of eternal death." Thus, the law reduces us to hopelessness, and drives us to surrender ourselves to God's mercy. In order to meet this situation, the lawgiver did not set aside the law and thus condone injustice; rather, he fully entered into the man who perfectly obeyed the law and yet was punished as one who had broken it as all others do. Christ has kept the law for us, and shares the reward for doing so with us. Again in a positive way, Calvin asserted, "The whole intention of the Law is to teach love"—love of God and love of neighbor. Though it is hard to keep the ten commandments, we are not thereby excused. The law instructs and stimulates us to our duty. Since a believer can never be certain that he has kept it entirely, or that he will not disobey it in the future, he must rely on God's forgiveness. Faith is both the acceptance of, and assent to, the relationship God has established with humans—through Jesus Christ and the doctrines of the Creed. Faith is acceptance of and reliance on God's promise.[35]

Is the Mosaic law, then, eternally valid? In the only exchange Calvin had with Jews (as far as we can tell), he replied, No. In support of that "no" he used one of the pre-Christian Jewish contentions that in the messianic age the law is automatically abrogated.[36] Basically, the law for Calvin is preparation for Christ, but it is still useful in governing a modern political entity such as Geneva.

On the negative side of things Calvin attacked Jews for their "misinterpretation" of scriptural passages that testify to Christian faith, and their "stubbornness . . . to the last ditch" in sticking to their traditional interpretation of the Bible. He was sure that this was a sign that God had struck them with blindness for "rejecting the light of heaven when [it was] presented to them [and thus having] kept themselves in voluntary darkness."[37]

Calvin also contended that though the law was "given for salvation, . . . the Jews made their covenant with God invalid at once, and have, by violation of the justice of the Law, called God's anger down even more upon them[selves]. . . . God's covenant [and] adoption [of] the sons of Abraham to himself has been to many the cause of a double destruction" since redemption "becomes twice harmful when it is profaned unjustly."

Although in his *Institutes* Calvin used Paul's chapters 9–11 of Romans in a relatively sympathetic way, in his later *Commentary* on Romans 11:28–32, and in the *Commentary* on Jeremiah 19:9, he concluded that the Jews' "greatest crime consisted in their lack of faith," and that the Jews' "impiety, ingratitude, and rebelliousness exceeded the crimes of all other nations." Therefore, it was not at all astonishing that God severely avenged himself.[38]

Calvin lumped together papists and Jews, and attributed the rise of Antichrist to the Jews. (By contrast Luther attributed it to the pope.)[39]

To the Jewish debater's question, "In what way was your Messiah the king of peace, when . . . from that time the world has not rested from wars?" Calvin replied (in part): "the fault does not stick elsewhere than [with Jews who] first among men, . . . showed by their obstinacy that they did not want peace with God."[40]

On another point that is relevant to some of our topical issues, both Calvin and Luther opposed Christians making pilgrimages to the holy land. Christians should instead focus their attention on the "heavenly Jerusalem" by contrast to Jewish this-worldliness.[41]

In the latter part of his life (1549 and 1550) when many Reformed Christians were being persecuted and living in exile, Calvin may have given some evidence of "a growing sense of the hidden community of fate shared by Christians and Jews in their homeless state of persecution." Three sermon quotations may indicate this tendency.

> When we see, then, that we are like the Jews, we feel we are like the Jews, we have a mirror for recognizing rebellion against God. But as it will [lead] to our being punished quite harshly, shall we be able to tell ourselves that not enough has been attempted, and that on our part we have shown ourselves incorrigibles up to the end? And so, when we read [Jer. 16:1–7], let us learn to condemn not the Jews but ourselves, and to realize that we are no better. . . .

> And even though we are not of the race of Abraham and of this people who were delivered out of Egypt, nevertheless . . . [because we represent that people,] this deliverance ought not ever leave our ears [Jer. 16:12–15].

> . . . if one makes comparison with those of whom the prophet speaks here [Lam. 1:1], one will find that we are perhaps much worse than those at that [former] time.[42]

One significant difference between Calvin and Luther with regard to our subject is that Calvin never produced writings that focused specifically on Jews (with the exception of the one exchange with "a Jew" that has been mentioned but which was never published by him). The other comments noted in this paper are scattered among his many writings and are not the focus of his theology. Moreover, he did believe in a theory of development wherein Judaism not only prepared the way for Christ but still provided politically and morally useful laws. He never advocated the use of force against Jews (as he did against Christian heretics), and did not make any effort to undermine the position of Jews still living in Germany or expanding numerically and economically in Polish and Lithuanian territories (where, incidentally, there was then a sizable community of Reformed Christians).[43]

It is impossible to go into the complexities of the Anabaptist movement, but a few of the ideas and tendencies in a short-lived South German and Austrian group deserve mention because they represent a totally different theological tradition. Some of these Anabaptists rejected both the authority the reformers gave to *sola scriptura* and the Catholics' shared authority of scripture and tradition. For these mystical Anabaptists, for example, Hans Denck, authority could not rest on any external source but only on the "inner Word." Denck resisted the concept of "external coercion in matters of faith" and sought religious tolerance—that rarity of the sixteenth century—and ecumenical dialogue, including that with Jews. He apparently was a universalist in his theology of salvation. Denck also rejected Luther's law-gospel dichotomy. This group of Anabaptists denied the usual understanding of the Trinity. Christ was a son of God, as are all men (though others in a lesser degree), who was a great exemplar and teacher. These Anabaptists put great emphasis on discipleship and martyrdom. It is not enough to believe that Christ died as an atonement for oneself; rather the pilgrim must suffer *with* Christ. Along with the popular medieval mystics, who appear to be the chief source of this Anabaptist movement, they believed that human cooperation with the divine presence in oneself is part of the salvation process.[44]

In addition, some Swiss Anabaptists were not as anti-Jewish as most Protestants because they relied primarily on the Hebrew scriptures and especially the five books of Moses, and were convinced that the history of ancient Israel should be the guide for a modern state. One man—Augustin Bader—even had a vision of a multi-religious society in which all faiths and peoples would live in harmony.[45]

One other small group needs a brief mention, though the variety of their views and the complications of their life situations deserve more.

These were the Christian-Hebraists, of whom the first half of the six-teenth century produced a goodly crop of excellent scholars, especially from among the Reformed churches. Many of these men began as hu-manists, influenced by Erasmus, with a scholarly interest in Hebrew of the same sort as those who had an interest in Greek. Jerome Friedman hypothesizes that disenchantment with their time and its crises led these men to study ancient languages as a way of recovering what they per-ceived as a better or simpler world than their own. They hoped the ancient sources could be used to reshape their own societies. (Christian-Hebraists were often fascinated with Kabbalah.)

Christian Hebrew scholars often "expressed a diminished faith in traditional Christian belief and practice," and of course this immediately raised fears and created antagonism on the part of the church leaders, whether Protestant or Catholic. As Friedman puts it, "the problem posed by Christian-Hebraica was that the scalpel used had a Jewish blade." And since anti-Judaism and antisemitism were so prevalent, "the integrity of anyone studying Hebrew would be questioned and compromised." All of them were accused of judaizing at one time or another, and it appears that they produced some anti-Jewish writings simply to prove that they also could be and were against the Jews. This seems particularly evident in the allegedly missionary treatises. Under such a cover the scholars were able to publish some of their most contro-versial works.

One of the most interesting of this group is Paul Fagius, who is called by Friedman a "Christian Pharisee." Fagius was centuries ahead of his time in being interested in the Pharisaic milieu from which Jesus and the apostles emerged, and in the Jewish origins of Christian prac-tices, beliefs, and prayers. He showed the congruence of New Testament ethics and the *Ethics of the Fathers,* and defended ancient Jewish piety, which "was not corrupted by the passage of time." (Nevertheless, he condemned the rabbis as blind and foolish, and the "dogma of the Talmud" as empty and stupid.)[46]

As we consider Jewish reactions to and evaluations of the Reforma-tion and its various leaders (the other side of our subject), we need to be aware that European Jewry was in a severe crisis situation. 1517, when Luther nailed his 95 Theses to the Wittenberg church door, was only twenty-five years after the largest, most learned, cultured and estab-lished Jewish community of Europe had been forced to choose between conversion to Christianity or expulsion from Spain; only nineteen years after a sizable portion of those who left Spain for Portugal were faced with a royal decree ordering conversion; and only eleven years after the 1506 massacre of Lisbon, the climax of a wave of pogroms against the "new Christians" (Jewish converts) of that country. The destruction of this centuries-old Iberian community virtually ended Jewish existence (as Jewish) in western Europe, since Jews had already been expelled from England, France, Sicily, southern Italy, and the Swiss cantons. In Central Europe there was no security and new pressures of antisemitism were felt in the small German principalities, the imperial cities, and other areas of the Holy Roman Empire where small Jewish communities still existed. As Gordon Rupp has put it, "the 16th century was a time when, for the Jewish people, the dim lights were going out, one by one, across Europe."[47]

Many Jews wondered whether this multitude of sufferings were signs of the Messiah's coming. In any case, given their critical situation, they naturally wondered about the meaning of the Reformation, the many conflicts to which it gave rise, and what implications it would have for their communities, for Judaism as a faith, and for God's plan of redemption. Earlier, in the fourteenth century, a Provence scholar had attributed Jewish suffering to the actions of some Jews who, in the first century, had transgressed by spreading Christianity among the Gentiles, and leading "multitudes without number" astray into this "folly." Exile would be prolonged, he maintained, until "we return to the Lord in complete penitence" and help others "back to the true faith" through Jewish missionary propagation.

Some of this type of thinking influenced Jewish responses both to the pre-Reformation Hussite movement in Bohemia, and then to the early Luther. His emergence and the vigor of the transformation taking place astonished many Jews and at first led to optimism: Messianic hopes were revived and 1524 was chosen as the messianic year of the beginning of the redemption by Rabbi Zacuto. Rabbi Joseph b. R. Joshua haKohen in Italy had no messianic expectations, nor any illusions that Luther was anything but a devout Christian, but he nevertheless saw value in the rejection of icons and worship of saints. It was a triumph of wisdom—and *tikkun*. He was also impressed by the heroism of the French reformers in Provence who remained firm in the face of "Catholic brutality." He hoped that the religious strife with all its sacrifices would ultimately bring toleration to the European kingdoms,[48] a hope that eventually proved partially correct.

In Germany itself, however, disenchantment soon set in. As Jews there witnessed Luther's growing absolutism, they realized that their own existence was more precarious. Even so, the ever-widening divisions within Christendom still seemed to presage a better time ahead. Rabbi Eliezer Ashkenazi interpreted his time as the "Generation of the Tower of Babel" with Christians seeking to create a "universal caliphate," absolute conformity, and no allowance for religious diversity. This was evil, and therefore God put division among them, for only in a mixed environment (what we would call pluralism) can an individual search for truth and attain it through free choice. Rabbi Eliezer believed that only truth arrived at by free choice had enduring value.[49]

A number of Jews interpreted the fragmentation of Christianity and the religious wars, as God's punishment of Christendom for its vilification, expulsion, and other forms of mistreatment of themselves, God's people. Abraham ben Eliezer Halevi, a Spanish Jew, saw the Reformation as a necessary crisis, following the terrible events of 1492, a crisis in which "Luther was God's agent sent to destroy corrupt Rome before the world's end."[50] Another rabbi worked out a chronology of redemption in which 1520–21 and Luther's early activities were the first stage: Luther was seen as a "crypto-Jew" whose revolt would "draw the gentiles near to the Jewish Religion and its laws." Rabbi Zacuto even thought of Luther as a Jew at heart, but using circumspection in order to be successful in winning the public to his views.[51]

Given the Jewish experiences in Catholic Europe, we might expect to find more silent cheering on behalf of Protestantism. Though this tended to be more the case among Spanish Jewish refugees and Marranos, several factors militated against it becoming the predominant position. Italian Jews were still benefitting from the Renaissance atmosphere; antisemitism had increased in Germany from about 1480 and the cities from which Jews were expelled were often Protestant. A negative association was made even when Protestants had not been around at the time of expulsion.[52] On some of the theological and ecclesiastical issues that mattered to Jews, their own views more often seemed closer to Catholicism. For example, Rabbi Yehiel of Pisa attacked the anti-freewill stance (and especially predestination) of the reformers, and supported the Catholics' pro-freewill position. Similarly he agreed with the Catholics on the merit of good works as against the Protestants' faith alone.

Rabbi Josel of Rosheim had excellent relations with Wolfgang Capito at Strasbourg, even attending some of his lectures and sermons, but when Martin Bucer attempted to compel Jewish attendance at sermons, and when he advised Philip of Hesse about how to deal with Jews there, Rabbi Josel went on the counter-offensive with his powers of persuasion. In a 1539 debate at Frankfurt, Bucer treated him so acrimoniously that Josel felt it necessary to say, "God . . . has perserved us since the days of Abraham and will doubtless, in His mercy, also preserve us from you in the future." When Luther published *On the Jews and Their Lies,* Rabbi Josel was able to persuade the Strasbourg city council to prohibit its being reprinted in the city (although he was unable to get them to prohibit its sale). He argued that "never has . . . any scholar [contended before] that we Jews ought to be treated with violence and such tyranny."[53] He turned to favoring Roman Catholicism more and more, seeing the old system as having better safeguards in it. He did not foresee, nor live to witness, the disastrous change in papal policy that Pope Paul IV initiated in 1555 when he forced Roman Jews into a ghetto, made Catholic toleration of Jewish existence dependent on Jews soon converting, burned Marranos and Jewish books.[54] Josel also saw Luther's reforms as inclining toward casting off the yoke of restraint, and pandering to the brutish instincts of the mob. The Luther of later years was viewed as a Haman, set to annihilate Jews by harsh measures and forced conversions.[55]

Did anything positive emerge from the Reformation with regard to Christian attitudes toward Jews and Judaism, or religious toleration and liberty? The interest in the Hebrew language and the Jewish literature to which it had given birth laid a foundation for a less biased understanding of Jewish faith to emerge eventually. Zwingli put forward a democratic concept of the church that would, when combined with other factors, contribute to a separation of church and state and freedom of conscience. John Calvin and his colleagues developed a branch of Christianity that had a deep appreciation of Hebrew scripture and biblical law/ "Teaching" (heretofore only regarded as "Jewish legalism," a "dead letter," or an instrument of condemnation). This positive attitude toward Torah and toward Israel would develop in the latter part of the sixteenth century and in the seventeenth century among Dutch and English millennarians and English puritans into a genuine interest in Jews as persons (though still with conversion as a goal).[56] In 1614, in Brandenburg [Germany], the Elector John Sigismund proclaimed liberty of conscience for his Christian subjects,[57] and in the 1630s Roger Williams founded the American colony of "Providence Plantation" in order to allow liberty of conscience to be practised by all, including Jews. As for Lutheranism, R. J. Zwi Werblowsky reminds us that the

Lutheran church conceives of Christianity as a life of reform. Therefore the contemporary repudiation of Luther's teachings on the Jews and Judaism makes the church *more* Lutheran!

NOTES

1. See T. H. L. Parker, *John Calvin,* p. 146; Luther, "An Admonition Against the Jews," in Heiko A. Oberman, *The Roots of Anti-Semitism,* p. 121. Luther warned the authorities, do "not make yourselves party to the sins of others" and incur God's wrath on account of the presence of Jews in your midst. If the Jews refuse to convert, "neither tolerate nor suffer their presence" (15 February 1546).

2. Cited in Salo Baron, *A Social and Religious History of the Jews,* XIII, p. 218, italics added. This view is repeated in various forms in many of Luther's writings, since it was so central to his theology and ecclesiology.

3. Baron, XIII, p. 219.

4. Paul Johnson, *A History of Christianity,* pp. 288–89.

5. *That Jesus Christ Was Born a Jew,* in *Luther's Works* (hereafter, *LW*), vol. 45, pp. 198, 200, 201, 229. The first half is a reply to accusations made by his opponents that he was teaching that Jesus was conceived by Joseph, that Mary was not a virgin, and that she had many sons after Christ.

6. However, Heinrich Bornkamm finds that Luther was going further than much of Christian tradition insofar as he asserted that the old covenant did *not* prepare for the new covenant. It was its absolute antithesis: "Law and gospel [Old and New Testaments] are deadly enemies"; so much so that a believer in the Old Testament "must beat Moses to death" in order to accept the new covenant. Bornkamm concludes that Luther thus Christianized the Old Testament and demolished the whole scheme of salvation history (*Heilsgeschichte*) as the early church interpreted it (*Luther and the Old Testament,* pp. 146, 254 [and citing Luther's *Table Talk,* 1532].

7. Oberman, *The Roots of Anti-Semitism,* pp. 46, 111.

8. Haim Hillel Ben-Sasson, "The Reformation in Contemporary Jewish Eyes," pp. 166–167.

9. Baron, XIII, p. 115: "Luther doubtless collaborated."

10. John W. Kleiner, *The Attitudes of the Strasbourg Reformers Toward Jews and Judaism,* p. 67.

11. Oberman, p. 120, citing Luther's letter to Josel dated June 11, 1537.

12. Jerome Friedman advises this course in *The Most Ancient Testimony,* p. 204.

13. *LW,* 47, p. 264.

14. Friedman, *The Most Ancient Testimony,* p. 204; and *On the Jews and Their Lies, LW,* 47, p. 149.

15. *LW,* 47, pp. 268–270, 285–288ff, 292.

16. Jules Isaac, *Jesus and Israel*, p. 249.

17. He was convinced that Jews were causing his ill-health as well as perverting Christianity and world order (letter to his wife, January 2, 1546, in Friedman, *The Most Ancient Testimony*, pp. 203, 210 n.1; and *LW*, 50, p. 290).

18. Gordon Rupp, "In the Context of His Life and Times," *Face to Face*, X (Spring 1983), p. 9.

19. Sermon published as "An Admonition Against the Jews," cited in Rupp, p. 10 (italics added).

20. Oberman, pp. 113–117.

21. Baron, XIII, pp. 228, 231, 232; Oberman, pp. 10, 47. However, Melanchthon sent a copy of *On the Jews and Their Lies* to Philip of Hesse with a comment about the useful lessons to be found in it (Baron, XIII, p. 231).

22. Baron, XIII, p. 228.

23. Betsy Halpern Amaru, "Martin Luther and Jewish Mirrors," *Jewish Social Studies*, XLVI 2 (Spring 1984), p. 96; Oberman, p. 49 (full quote on p. 137, n. 64).

24. Baron, XIII, p. 229; Friedman, *The Most Ancient Testimony*, p. 204.

25. Sholom Singer, *Jews, Luther and the Reformation*, p. 11

26. Baron, XIII, p. 222. See S. Bernhard Erling, "Martin Luther and the Jews in the Light of His Lectures on Genesis," *Immanuel* [Jerusalem] 18 (Fall 1984):64–78.

27. *LW*, 47, p. 280.

28. Oberman, pp. 49, 64 n.137, citing *Weimarer Ausgabe, Abteilung Werke*, 50:323, 324, 8.

29. Rupp, p. 6; Oberman, pp. 47–49.

30. Baron, XIII, p. 236.

31. Baron, XIII, p. 238.

32. John Kleiner, *The Attitudes of the Strasbourg Reformers*, pp. 244, 245, 251, 252, 227, citing Bucer.

33. Kleiner, pp. 266, 265; Baron, XIII, p. 241.

34. In 1632, in Geneva, a pastor was strangled for apostasy and conversion to Judaism (Jules Isaac, *Jesus and Israel*, p. 249).

35. Parker, *John Calvin*, pp. 44–45, 46.

36. Calvin was responding to the Jewish challenger's use of Matthew 5:17: "I am come not to destroy but to fulfill [the Law]" (Baron XIII, p. 290).

37. Baron, XIII, pp. 148–49, 291.

38. Baron, XIII, pp. 287–288.

39. Baron, XIII, p. 287; Oberman, p. 108; and many passages in Luther's writings.

40. Jean Calvin, Question VIII and response, *Ad Quaestiones et Objecta Iudaei Cuisusdam Responsio* (Response to Questions and Objections of a Certain Jew), in *Opera*, IX, pp. 653–746. I am indebted to Dr. Michael A. Ryan for this document and its translation.

41. Mordechai S. Chertoff, "Jerusalem in Song and Psalm," in Alice L. Eckardt, ed., *Jerusalem: City of the Ages* (Washington, D.C., 1986), p. 226.

42. Oberman, p. 141; sermons, July 8, 1549, September 6, 1550; cited p. 144, n.6. Translation provided by Dr. Edna de Angeli.

43. Baron, XIII, pp. 291, 462 n.100; and "John Calvin and the Jews," p. 159.

44. Werner O. Packull, *Mysticism and the Early South German-Austrian Anabaptist Movement, 1525–1531,* pp. 40, 44, 49–50, 159, 176, 178, 179–180. Such a belief in divine-human cooperation shares an affinity with Judaism.

45. Baron, XIII, p. 244.

46. Friedman, *The Most Ancient Testimony,* pp. 5, 100, 115, 116, 214, 260, 261, 244.

47. Through the fifteenth century and up until 1519 urban expulsions in the German Empire were extensive. After 1520 they were relatively few (Oberman, p. 93); Rupp, p. 4.

48. Haim Hillel Ben-Sasson, "The Reformation in Contemporary Jewish Eyes," pp. 244, 263 n.78, 277, 283.

49. Friedman, *The Most Ancient Testimony,* p. 257; Ben-Sasson, "The Reformation . . . ," pp. 258–59, 315.

50. Friedman, "The Reformation in Alien Eyes," p. 32. Halevi saw all the good things he wanted to see in Luther's *That Jesus Christ Was Born a Jew:* that Jews had rightly resisted Catholicism; that to be a good Christian one had almost to become a Jew; that Catholics could call him (Luther) a Jew if they tired of calling him a heretic.

51. Gershom Scholem, cited in Ben-Sasson, "The Reformation in . . . ," p. 264. The view of Luther as anti-Christian was based on his iconoclasticism and detestation of priests (266–267).

52. We must realize that there was only a very small German Jewish population then—probably only a few hundred in all Germany, the largest, Frankfurt, having about 78 (Kleiner, pp. 43–44).

53. Ben-Sasson, "The Reformation in . . . ," pp. 287–288.

54. Kenneth R. Stow, *Catholic Thought and Papal Jewry Policy 1555–1593* (New York: The Jewish Theological Seminary of America and Ktav, 1977); Paul Johnson, *A History of the Jews,* pp. 243–244.

55. Not all rabbis reached this conclusion. Rabbi Hayyim b. R. Bazalel believed that the reformers' search for truth might make a rapprochement with Judaism possible, whereas Catholicism's asceticism was totally un-Jewish (Ben-Sasson, "The Reformation in . . . ," p. 298).

56. Among some twentieth-century Evangelicals—not to mention mainline Protestants—this appreciation would go much further and even eliminate the conversionist emphasis.

57. D. Clair Davis, "The Reformed Church of Germany," in W. Stanford Reid, ed., *John Calvin: His Influence in the Western World,* p. 83.

REFERENCES AND BIBLIOGRAPHY

Baron, Salo. "John Calvin and the Jews," *Harry A. Wolfson Jubilee Volume*. Jerusalem: American Academy for Jewish Research, 1965, pp. 141–158.

———. *A Social and Religious History of the Jews*. Second Edition, Vols. XIII, XIV. New York: Columbia University Press, 1953–1969.

Ben-Sasson, Haim Hillel. *A History of the Jewish People*. Cambridge: Harvard University Press, 1976.

———. "The Reformation in Contemporary Jewish Eyes," in *Proceedings of the Israel Academy of Sciences and Humanities*, IV: 12, pp. 241–326. Jerusalem, 1971.

Bornkamm, Heinrich. *Luther and the Old Testament*. Trans. Eric and Ruth Gritsch; Victor I. Gruhn, ed. Philadelphia: Fortress Press, 1969.

Calvin, Jean, *Ad Quaestiones et Objecta Iudaei Cuisusdam Responsio* (Response to Questions and Objections of a Certain Jew), in *Opera*, IX, 653–674.

Cooperman, Bernard, ed. *Jewish Thought in the Sixteenth Century*. Cambridge: Harvard University Press, 1982.

Davis, D. Clair. "The Reformed Church of Germany," in W. Stanford Reid, ed. *John Calvin: His Influence in the Western World*. Grand Rapids: Zondervan Publishing, 1982, pp. 123–40.

Dickens, A. G. *Reformation and Society in Sixteenth Century Europe*. London: Thames & Hudson, 1966.

Erling, S. Bernhard. "Martin Luther and the Jews in the Light of His Lectures on Genesis," *Immanuel* [Jerusalem], 18 (Fall 1984): 64–78.

Friedman, Jerome. *The Most Ancient Testimony: Sixteenth-Century Christian Hebraica in the Age of Renaissance Nostalgia*. Athens, OH: Ohio University Press, 1983.

———. "The Reformation in Alien Eyes," *The Sixteenth Century Journal*, XIV, 1 (1983):23–39.

———. "Sebastian Münster, the Jewish Mission and Protestant Anti-semitism," *Archiv für Reformationsgeschichte* 70 (1979): 238–59.

Gutteridge, Richard. "Luther and the Jews," Appendix I, *Open Thy Mouth for the Dumb: The German Evangelical Church and the Jews, 1879–1950*. Oxford: Basil Blackwell, 1976.

Halpern Amaru, Betsy. "Martin Luther and Jewish Mirrors," *Jewish Social Studies*, XLVI 2 (Spring, 1984): 95–102.

Isaac, Jules. *Jesus and Israel.* New York: Holt, Rinehart and Winston, 1971.

Johnson, Paul. *A History of Christianity.* London: Weidenfeld and Nicolson, 1976.

————. *A History of the Jews.* London: Weidenfeld and Nicholson, 1987.

Kleiner, John W. "The Attitudes of the Strasbourg Reformers Toward Jews and Judaism." Ph.D. thesis, Philadelphia: Temple University, 1982.

Luther's Works, Vol. 45, Walther I. Brandt, ed. Philadelphia: Muhlenberg Press, 1962.

————, Vol. 47, Franklin Sherman, ed. Philadelphia: Fortress Press, 1971.

"Martin Luther and the Jews," *Face to Face,* X (Spring 1983).

Newman, Louis Israel. *Jewish Influence on Christian Reform Movements.* New York: Columbia University Press, 1925.

Oberman, Heiko A. *The Roots of Anti-Semitism in the Age of Renaissance and Reformation.* Trans. James I. Porter. Philadelphia: Fortress Press, 1984.

Packull, Werner O. *Mysticism and the Early South German-Austrian Anabaptist Movement, 1525–1531.* Scottsdale, PA: Herald Press, 1977.

Parker, T. H. L. *John Calvin.* Tring, Eng.: Lion Publishing, 1977.

Raitt, Jill, ed. *Shapers of Religious Traditions in Germany, Switzerland, and Poland, 1560–1600.* New Haven and London: Yale University Press, 1981.

Reid, W. Stanford, ed. *John Calvin: His Influence in the Western World.* Grand Rapids: Zondervan Publishing House, 1982.

Rupp, Gordon. "In the Context of His Life and Times," *Face to Face,* X (Spring 1983): 4–10.

Shiels, W. J., ed. *Persecution and Toleration.* Oxford: Basil Blackwell, 1984.

Siirala, Aarne. "Reflections from a Lutheran Perspective," in Eva Fleischner, ed. *Auschwitz: Beginning of a New Era?* New York: Ktav, 1977, pp. 135–48.

————. "A Theological Analysis," *Face to Face,* X (Spring 1983): 11–21.

Scult, Mel. *Millennial Expectations and Jewish Liberties: A Study of the Efforts to Convert the Jews in Britain, up to the Mid Nineteenth Century.* Leiden: E. J. Brill, 1978.

Singer, Sholom. *Jews, Luther, and the Reformation.* Oxford: Oxford Centre for Postgraduate Hebrew Studies, 1980.

Steinmetz, David. *Reformers in the Wings.* Philadelphia: Fortress Press, 1971. (Chapter 19: "Hans Denck")

Toon, Peter, ed. *Puritans, the Millennium and the Future of Israel: Puritan Eschatology 1600 to 1660.* Cambridge & London: James Clarke & Co., 1970.

Van Den Berg, J. "The Eschatological Expectation of Seventeenth Century Dutch Protestantism with Regard to the Jewish People," in Peter Toon, ed., *Puritans, the Millennium and the Future of Israel,* pp. 137–53.

Worden, Blair. "Toleration and the Cromwellian Protectorate," in W. J. Shiels, ed., *Persecution and Toleration,* pp. 199–234.

The Enlightenment and Western Religion

Arthur Hertzberg

Let me begin with an imaginary conversation which could have taken place but did not. In the latter part of the seventeenth century, two great scholars lived in the city of Metz in eastern France. The rabbi of the Jewish community was Joshua Falk, who was one of the greatest figures in rabbinic scholarship in recent centuries; the bishop was the famous Jacques Benigne Bossuet, who was the most important Christian theologian in France of that era. There is no record in either Jewish or Christian sources that they ever met, though it is possible that they did, for Metz was in a border area, and it had very recently been acquired by the French. Jewish rights in the city were far from secure, and it is therefore possible that the rabbi did go as supplicant to the bishop on occasion. The greater likelihood is that the Jewish community conducted its business with the military governor of the city and that Jews lived in total isolation from the local Catholic hierarchy.

Even if Falk and Bossuet did meet, they had nothing to talk about. Intellectual and theological encounters between Jews and Christians throughout the Middle Ages (and the Middle Ages were still alive in eastern France in the seventeenth century, at least in relationship to Jews) had occurred, on occasion, in literature, when Christian scholars such as Aquinas had read and quoted Maimonides. When rabbis and prelates met in person to discuss religion, it was usually in the tragic high drama of theological disputations to which Jews were summoned, and in which they could only lose.

The converse is also true: Christianity as a religion was not ever a major theological concern for medieval Judaism. Left to themselves, without the historic pressure of the Christian majority on the Jews of the

134

west, Christianity would have been ignored. To the degree to which it was discussed by Jewish thinkers of the medieval era, such considerations arose out of the necessities of keeping Jews from converting under the pressure of persecution and of providing some formulas of grudging respect which would satisfy Christian critics, who kept insisting that the essence of Judaism was its unrelieved hatred of Christianity.

At about the time that Bossuet and Falk were living in Metz, the most important divine in the New World was Cotton Mather. His contemporaries regarded him, correctly, as the greatest intellect to have appeared in the American colonies. In 1697, or thereabouts, Cotton Mather persuaded himself that he understood the Hebrew Bible better than the Jews, who had been engaged for many centuries in avoiding the "truth" that God's revelation to them prefigured and announced through his ultimate incarnation in Jesus. Mather was very much a millennarian; that is, he believed the end of days was near and that it could be brought nearer by the conversion of the Jews. He therefore wrote a book to demonstrate the truth of Christianity from a "correct" interpretation of many verses of the Hebrew Bible, without invoking a single passage from the New Testament. Mather had heard that there were a few Jews in Carolina, and so he sent this book southward in order to convert them with incontrovertible arguments from their own scripture. The effort failed, for the Jews in Carolina either remained obstinate, or, more probably, were simply not interested. And so, if Mather had ever traveled to Metz, there would nonetheless have been no meeting of Catholic-Protestant-Jew. Bossuet would have had no time for a Protestant, for this heresy was then proscribed in France, and both Bossuet and Mather would have seen Rabbi Falk as only the most obdurate of all possible candidates for conversion.

This centuries-old abyss between Judaism and Christianity was not bridged, on either side, out of inner necessity, out of theological developments which arose within each of the traditions. The Jewish-Christian dialogue was made necessary by the Enlightenment and by the French and American Revolutions.

While Rabbi Falk and Bishop Bossuet were not talking to each other in Metz, an ex-student in the Yeshivah, the school of Talmud, in Amsterdam, named Baruch Spinoza was writing one of the most revolutionary of all books, his *Theological-Political Tractate*. His essential assertion was that both Judaism and Christianity were, at their best, imperfect reflections of the truths that were available in their fullness only through universal reason. Within a century, this heresy had become the dominant opinion of the educated class in Europe and America. The result of this historic change in the climate of opinion was the separation of church and state. This profound reordering of society was enacted by both of the great political revolutions which occurred at the end of the eighteenth century. The modern era which began, for state and society, with these two great cataclysms was to be marked everywhere by moving religion formally away from the center of society, from its previous role as organizing principle, to the margin. Individuals were now free to believe or not to believe, to associate or not to associate with the institutions of any of the faiths, but the modern state exercised no pressure for religion or in behalf of any of the faiths.

It is within this new climate that Judaism and Christianity began their dialogue. Since the various faiths were now equal before the law, they were now lumped together by civic authority. In some of the early dramas of the French Revolution, priests, ministers, and rabbis marched together in parades to mark the adoption in 1791 of the first French constitution. Two years earlier, when the new republican government of the United States had begun, comparable scenes had been enacted. The rabbi in New York had even participated, along with other clergy, in the ceremony in which George Washington had been inaugurated President. Such a scene could never have happened at coronations of French kings or of English monarchs, while the older relations between the faiths still obtained.

I do not know what the clergy talked about at these unprecedented functions, as they marched together, but I suspect that they passed the time discussing the immediate political scene rather than in creating a new theology for the Jewish-Christian encounter. Parades hardly lend themselves to such deliberations, and especially not when such moments of drama occur in the midst of dangerous times. Nonetheless, these marches were important. The new, secular state was forcing the religions to encounter each other and to establish a new relationship, not only with the state, but also among themselves.

I cannot leave these considerations of history without making one more observation: on balance, Jews liked the new regime; Christians did not. The triumph of the secular state radically lessened the role of Christianity in society. The established church was everywhere a major loser, and nowhere as dramatically, and even as tragically, as in France, the "home of the Revolution" in Europe. At least in its Catholic version, Christianity throughout the nineteenth century and into the twentieth remained opposed to "modernism," that is, to the removal of the church from its centrality in society, and to forcing it to behave as a mere equal to Christian heretics, Jews, and even unbelievers. For Jews, the new secularism did bring a major threat to the faith, for wherever they could, Jews rushed in their many thousands into the secular schools. Some Jews very rapidly became part of the most "advanced" intelligentsia. This danger to the faith was understood early; it was deplored and fought, but even the bulk of the Orthodox gladly accepted the new political era, for it brought them economic equality and it allowed them, for the first time since the diaspora had begun some eighteen centuries earlier, to live in society and not on its margins.

Christianity as a whole thus confronted modernity with mixed feelings, more negative than positive, while Jews hailed the secular revolutions as times of liberation. Christianity as organized faith was the big loser in the French and American Revolutions; Judaism was essentially the big winner, for it now was, for the first time in the west, no worse off than anyone else.

Jews were of no consequence among the makers of the American and French Revolutions. Both of these cataclysms would have occurred in precisely the same form if there had not been a single Jew in either the American colonies or France. But, for reasons which are obvious in the light of what I have just said, Jews were almost instantly major partisans of these revolutions, and so they have remained to this very day. In America today Jews are the only religious community which remains unwaveringly, and almost unanimously, devoted to strict construction of the First Amendment. The Christian majority in America, in all its parts, is overwhelmingly for some form of prayer in the public schools; Jews are against such prayers. Why? Because they find in the First Amendment protection of their equality, that is, of their right to live in society free of the pressure that is inevitably exerted on the minority by the religio-cultural traditions of the majority.

It is no accident at all that throughout the nineteenth century and into the twentieth some of the greatest minds of Jewish origin followed after Spinoza in being against tradition, in wanting to dynamite the western past and to recreate society on a new foundation. Spinoza invoked universal reason; Karl Marx declared all men to be alike in their deepest relations which, as he insisted, were determined by economic concerns; in due course Freud declared that, in his ultimate interior history, man was a battleground between instinct and conscience, and that social clashes would disappear if the inner disorders were cured. The thread that runs through all of these theories is one that each of these three seminal figures of modernity acknowledged in his work, and not even very obliquely: in the new world of Messiah on this earth, the painful, continuing threat of antisemitism would disappear, for its basis in unreason, or class conflict, or religious myth-making would have disappeared. The bulk of the Jewish community, and certainly the representatives of the Jewish religion, opposed all three of these heretics, but these names continue to be cited as a kind of litany of great "Jewish contributions to western culture" by people who do not know much about either Judaism or Jewish history—but there is nonetheless some truth in the proposition that these thinkers arose in part out of the Jewish situation in the pre-modern world. All three were reacting to the persistence of Jew-hatred, and each was trying to find a cure to this disease of western culture.

Having said all this, it is nonetheless true that, even in the Jewish agenda, the Enlightenment and what followed after in the political history of the west was far from an unmixed blessing for Jews. The obvious problem, of the survival of the faith in the new open society, has already been mentioned in passing, but it must now be dealt with more directly. At the very dawn of the French Revolution, when the *cahiers* were being prepared for the delegates to the Etats Généraux that Louis XVI had convoked, the Jews requested equality of economic rights, but they did not imagine the abolition of the separate Jewish community. In France they came around to this view only in the turmoil of the Revolution, and not without some reluctance. The issue was clearer still a few years later in Holland, when the revolutionary Batavian Republic was being created. The leaders of the organized Jewish community argued formally and publicly before the Constitutional Assembly that the Jews be allowed to maintain their separate existence and that they not be integrated totally into the new political structure. It was better to forgo the right to vote and hold public office, if thereby the coercive power of the organized Jewish community over individual Jews could be preserved. The faith would be more secure. In mid-nineteenth century central Europe, Rabbi Moses Schreiber, who had come from Frankfurt to be the rabbi in Bratislava (a town in easy distance of the ever more secular Vienna), thundered that all innovations were forbidden by scripture. By fiat and will he created a Jewish ghetto in which his community lived as if they were still in the sixteenth century. These counterattacks on modernity did not prevail, but they were not as unimportant as so many of those who write about modern Jewish history have made them out to be. Jews knew that modernity was not good for the ancestral faith.

A more important threat came from the very equality among the religions which the Enlightenment had defined. All religions had been praised by Voltaire, amidst his repetitive loud damns, as being equally valid paths to virtue. A much more pro-religious figure of the Enlightenment in Germany, Gotthold Lessing, had written a play, *Nathan the Wise,* to make the same point through the parable of three rings. Each of them was equally genuine, or equally contrived; they were the inheritance that the ultimate Father had left to his Catholic, Protestant, and Jewish sons, until he perhaps would tell them at the end of time which of the three rings was the original. If there was no substantial difference among religions, it was possible for some Jews to argue that it would serve their purpose better to find virtue through Christianity. If the symbols and rituals of the various faiths were accidents of history, those who wanted to enter the new age could move freely, and even in good conscience, to the religious camp of the majority. This cost of avoiding antisemitism was more than worth it. Therefore, throughout the nineteenth century, there were thousands of conversions to Christianity by Jews, such as Karl Marx's father and Heinrich Heine, who did not believe either religion very much. Many thousands more simply assimilated into the dominant culture without undergoing any conversion rituals. Political and economic equality did not come cheap.

This problem had been foreshadowed in the earliest days of the French Revolution. The more moderate side of the Enlightenment had offered the Jews equality but, in return, they had been asked to assimilate. In the first debate, in December of 1789, of the Jewish question in the Parliament which made the French Revolution, Count Stanislas de Clermont-Tonnerre had asserted that "one must refuse everything to the Jews as a nation, but one must give them everything as individuals. They must become citizens."[1] In his view, there could not be "a nation within a nation." Clermont-Tonnerre went on to insist that the Jews must abandon their separatist traditions and melt into the majority; if they refused to do so, then they should all be forced to move to Palestine. In actual practice, of course, and especially in more pragmatic, and untidy, English-speaking countries, the grant of legal equality did not come with any overt demands that Jews assimilate—but there was a suggestion that entering freedom required a Jew to rethink his identity even more fundamentally than Christians had to rethink their Christianity. No one ever suggested that Christian old-believers should be shipped to the holy land.

The far greater calamity for Jews was the other, more doctrinaire element of the Enlightenment, which wanted to remake society according to ideological plan. The dominant idea of the Enlightenment was that men could be remade, but, as some of the greatest figures of the eighteenth century insisted, some men were hopelessly flawed and beyond redemption. They were by nature incapable of being reformed, and indeed, if they are given equality and freedom, this would simply give unbridled scope to their obnoxious and destructive nature. The leader of this opinion was Voltaire. He though that blacks were less than human, and he was particularly venomous in his assessment of Jews. They were the enemies of mankind: "they are born with fanaticism in their hearts as Bretons are born blond."[2] Their "genetic nature" was both dangerous and irreversible. This opinion was the root of the most searing problem that the Enlightenment brought Jews: it ushered in a new form of antisemitism that was more ferocious and deadlier than the medieval Christian variety, because a new *raison d'être* had been constructed for Jew-hatred. The Jews were now defined as a threatening disease. No matter what they did, no matter how they might try to remake themselves, the bulk of the Jews, and probably all of them, would remain "enemies of the human race." This fateful declaration was the root of modern racism. If it was possible in the eighteenth century for civilized gentlemen to live off of the misery of black slaves, while talking of the equality of all mankind, Nazis who played Bach would eventually talk of a new order while they burned Jews at Auschwitz.

The account of Jews and of Judaism with the Enlightenment is thus far more complicated than it appears to be at first glance. It is only at its least ideological, in the thinking of Montesquieu in France and of the British Whigs, that the Enlightenment has offered true and lasting hope for mankind. We should have learned by now, two centuries after the American and the French Revolutions, and two generations after the Bolshevik Revolution, that ideologies which promise to bring the Messiah on this earth are false. The end of the days will come in God's good time, when he chooses, and as an act of grace; those who would force his hand have invariably murdered men and women who do not fit their visions, and, what is worse, they have committed such crimes in good conscience. People should not be "regenerated," according to someone else's prescription of what is good for them, and group identities should not be reformed to be parallel to one another in some tidy structure that an ideologue imagines. Freedom and decency are safe only in an untidy society in which individuals and groups are pressured as little as possible by the absolutes of other people.

Jews and Christians can sit down together, because we have been forced together by the Enlightenment. It uttered the demand that made our ancient traditions reformulate their way of living in society, so that we each could accommodate to a world in which it was neither dominant, as the Christians had been, nor uniquely marginal, as the Jews had been. We are also here because we are frightened of the Pandora's box that the most ideological element of the Enlightenment opened: unrestrainable racial hatred. We have come together to rethink some basic elements of the recent past, but not primarily for the sake of pure scholarship. We are here at a conference to act together in hope of lessening hatreds and avoiding the overwhelming tragedies.

Let us return, therefore, to the imaginary conversation with which I began these reflections. Let us imagine that Rabbi Falk, Bishop Bossuet, Dr. Mather, and Baruch Spinoza had sat down together, or are perhaps sitting down together now somewhere in the empyrean. What would they be saying to each other? I suspect that it would make a difference whether the conversation had been held in its own time, in the seventeenth century, or whether these men of great intellect and piety (each toward his own truth) were talking today, three hundred years later. In their own day, each would have argued that all of mankind would soon come to true enlightenment, that the scales would fall from all eyes, and that the truth of his own particular ideology would shine triumphant over all the world. Those were still optimistic times. I suspect that if this conversation was going on now, the four protagonists would still remain convinced of their respective beliefs, but the sobering realities of the intervening years would have made a difference. They would know that the distance between the dream of perfection and achieving it in this world is far greater than they had imagined, and that in the wars of Gog and Magog the forces of darkness often triumph, and remain in power for very long times. I suspect that they would be saying today that all we have to protect us is a fabric of civility, for which we are responsible together. That civility offers the only hope for the survival of society.

John Courtney Murray once said that pluralism is against the will of God, but that it is the only way for the city of man to survive. The meaning of interfaith relations in our day is that we must work together to protect the city of man, for it is gravely endangered by all the horrors which man has devised. If the city of man destroys itself, God is homeless.

NOTES

1. See A. Hertzberg, *The French Enlightenment and the Jews* (New York, 1968) 360–61.

2. Voltaire, *Oeuvres Complètes* (Moland Edition, XXXVIII) 439–40. See Hertzberg, *op. cit.*, Chapter 9.

Epilogue

Eugene J. Fisher

This volume of historical studies of the ancient Jewish-Christian relationship stops at the brink of the modern age, the century which Pope John Paul II has called "the century of the Shoah," and the century which has seen the rebirth of a Jewish state in the land of Israel after nearly two thousand years of exile. The significance of those two events, the Holocaust and the modern state of Israel, in themselves and as indicators of the present status of Jewish-Christian dialogue, will be the topic of the second volume of this two-volume set. That second volume will present extended essays by four of the most important thinkers, Jewish and Christian, in the field today.

In the meantime, the following outline of what I have called the "six stages" of Christian-Jewish relations through history may serve to summarize this volume and to set the stage for reflection on where we Jews and Christians may go from here in dialogue in the light of our long history.

1. The first stage is the briefest, encompassing the period from Jesus' ministry to the destruction of the Jerusalem Temple by the Romans in the year 70 of the first century of the common era. In this period, Christianity is perhaps best understood as a Jewish movement, although one can see the beginnings of its distinctive liturgical life reflected in the writings of St. Paul.[1]

2. The second stage may be called "the parting of ways," a phenomenon that took place gradually, reaching maturity and definitiveness by the middle of the fourth century. This was the period that saw the setting

down of the bulk of the New Testament, including the four gospels and the later epistles, such as the epistle to the Hebrews. During this stage many of the New Testament and patristic polemics against Jews and Judaism were written (against, for example, the Pharisees and the Temple cult), reflecting the confrontations between the emerging church and the developing rabbinic tradition. By contrast, the Mishnah, the earliest and "core" volume of the Talmud, was written at the end of the second century and, for its part, contains remarkably little anti-Christian polemic.[2]

3. The third stage begins at the end of the fourth century with the establishment of Christianity as the official religion of the Roman Empire. It ends in the tenth century with the massive violence perpetrated against the helpless Jewish communities of Christian Europe by the Crusaders (despite the strong opposition of the pope and Saint Bernard). In consolidating its secular power, church policy sought on the one hand to suppress the attractiveness of Judaism to potential converts and on the other to protect its existence, as a witness to the validity of the Hebrew Bible upon which the Christian proclamation is based. No such protection was accorded pagans, Muslims, or those deemed by the church to be heretical.[3]

4. The fourth stage, from the tenth through the sixteenth centuries, marks in a sense the nadir of Jewish-Christian relations. During this period, the teaching of contempt against Jews and Judaism, initially only theoretical, came to fruition in such tragic Christian acts against Jews as forced exiles and baptisms, ghettos, Talmud burnings, and blood libels. By the end of this period the Jewish communities of western Europe were decimated and severely oppressed.[4]

5. The fifth stage lasts from the Enlightenment to the eve of World War II. Though freed from the ghettos and contributing significantly to European culture and society, Jews were still considered "outsiders" by much of European society. Simultaneously, this period saw the development of pseudo-scientific racism, in great part as a means of rationalizing colonization and the slave trade to the New World. These "racialist" theories sought to justify what was being done to native peoples on the grounds that they were lower forms of humanity and were soon extended to the most "alien" group within Europe,

namely, the Jews. Nazism carried these theories to their most extreme to "justify" the Holocaust in which, ultimately, two-thirds of the Jews of Europe were coldly and systematically murdered. The Holocaust, therefore, represents a crisis not only for church teaching but for western civilization as a whole.[5]

6. The sixth stage begins with the liberation of the death camps by the Allied armies, and with the shock of realizing what had happened there. A high point was reached when a Jewish state was reestablished in the land of Israel, manifesting the Jewish people's renewed ability to hope. This spirit of hope for the future continued as the church began to embark upon a profound examination of conscience and renewal, resulting in *Nostra Aetate* and similar statements by other churches.[6]

The progress of the churches in addressing and reviewing their own teaching since Vatican II has been remarkable, as has been the intensity of the dialogue between Christians and Jews. In most respects, American Christians and Jews have been at the leading edge of the dialogue today. Central to and reflective of this dialogue have been several books worth noting. In 1980 the Stimulus Foundation published a volume honoring the 15th anniversary of *Nostra Aetate*. The book, *Biblical Studies: Meeting Ground of Jews and Christians* (Paulist Press), was edited by Lawrence Boadt, Helga Croner and Leon Klenicki. In 1987, Rabbi A. James Rudin and I put out a volume entitled *Twenty Years of Jewish-Catholic Relations* (Paulist). In 1988, the International Catholic-Jewish dialogue published its papers in a volume entitled *Fifteen Years of Catholic-Jewish Dialogue (1970–1985)* (Libreria Editrice Vaticana/Lateranaense).

Still, we in America have much to learn. Recently, for example, the bishops of Italy announced a national day of reflection on Catholic-Jewish relations, to involve all seminaries, Catholic schools, religious education classes, and adult groups. So far as I know, such a measure has no precedence at the national level, though several dioceses in America have launched similar efforts over the years. Today the necessary documents and official statements have come forth from the international, national and local levels. However, this great vision remains to be fully implemented in the lives of our Christian people. Here in America, where we are blessed with such active and faithful Jewish and Christian communities, we can do no less than continue this critical encounter.

NOTES

1. Cf., E. Fisher, ed., *The Jewish Roots of Christian Liturgy* (Paulist Press, Mahwah, NJ, 1990). Philip Cunningham, *Jewish Apostle to the Gentiles,* (Twenty-Third Publications, Mystic, CT, 1987).

2. Cf., E. Fisher and L. Klenicki, eds., *Root and Branches: Biblical Judaism, Rabbinic Judaism and Early Christianity* (St. Mary's Press, Winona, MN, 1987).

3. Cf., Edward A. Synan, *The Popes and the Jews in the Middle Ages* (Macmillan, New York, 1965).

4. Cf., Edward H. Flannery, *The Anguish of the Jews* (Paulist Press, A Stimulus Book, New York, 1985).

5. Cf., Heiko Oberman, *The Roots of Anti-Semitism in the Age of Renaissance and Reformation* (Fortress Press, Philadelphia, 1984). Also, E. Fisher, "The Church and Racism: Educational Implications" in *Professional Approaches for Christian Educators,* 1990. Also, *The Church and Racism: Towards A More Fraternal Society* (Pontifical Council for Justice and Peace, Vatican City, 1989).

6. Helga Croner, Compiler, *Stepping Stones to Further Jewish-Christian Relations,* and *More Stepping Stones to Jewish-Christian Relations: An Unabridged Collection of Christian Documents, 1975–1983* (Paulist Press—A Stimulus Book, New York, 1977 and 1985). Also, E. Fisher and L. Klenicki, *In Our Time: The Flowering of Jewish-Catholic Dialogue* (Paulist Press, A Stimulus Book, 1990).

Notes on the Contributors

JEREMY COHEN teaches Jewish history at Tel Áviv University and at The Ohio State University, where he holds the Samuel and Esther Melton Chair of Jewish History. His publications include *The Friars and the Jews: The Evolution of Medieval Anti-Judaism,* winner of the National Jewish Book Award, and *Essential Papers on Judaism and Christianity in Conflict: From Late Antiquity until the Reformation.*

MICHAEL J. COOK is Professor of Early Christian Literature at Hebrew Union College, Cincinnati. His recent publications include: "The Mission to Jews in Acts: Unraveling Luke's 'Myth of the Myriads'," in *Luke-Acts and the Jewish People,* ed. J. Tyson (Minneapolis, 1988); "The Ties That Blind: II Corinthians 3," in *When Jews and Christians Meet,* ed. J. Petuchowski (Albany, 1988); "Jewish Appraisals of Paul," in *Proceedings of the Center for Jewish-Christian Learning* 4 (1989).

ALICE L. ECKARDT is Professor Emerita of Religion Studies, Lehigh University; a Maxwell Fellow in the Study and Teaching of the Holocaust, Oxford Centre for Postgraduate Hebrew Studies (1989–90); co-author of *Long Night's Journey into Day: A Revised Retrospective on the Holocaust* (Wayne State University Press, 1988); editor-contributor of *Jerusalem: City of the Ages* (University Press of America, 1987); member and past-chairperson of the Christian Study Group on Judaism and the Jewish People; member of executive committee of the 1988 international conference "Remembering for the Future"; editorial board of *Holocaust and Genocide Studies.*

DR. EUGENE FISHER is the Executive Director of the Secretariat for Catholic-Jewish Relations, National Conference of Catholic Bishops. A leading international advocate of dialogue, his efforts have implemented far-reaching changes in the life of the church, its teaching and practice. He is author or editor of numerous volumes, including *Faith Without Prejudice* (1977); *Twenty Years of Jewish-Catholic Relations* (1986); and *Jewish Roots of Christian Liturgy* (1990). He is a Consultor to the Holy See's Commission for Religious Relations with the Jewish People and a member of the International Catholic-Jewish Liaison Committee.

JOHN G. GAGER is Professor of Religion at Princeton University and author of *Moses in Greco-Roman Paganism, Kingdom and Community: The Social World of Early Christianity,* and *The Origins of Anti-Semitism: Attitudes toward Judaism in Pagan and Christian Antiquity.*

FATHER DANIEL J. HARRINGTON S.J. is Professor of New Testament at Weston School of Theology, Cambridge, MA, and editor of *New Testament Abstracts.* A past president of the Catholic Biblical Association, he has written extensively on Second Temple Judaism and the New Testament. His recent books on John (1990) and Matthew (1990) pay particular attention to the significance of those texts for Christian-Jewish relations in antiquity and today.

ARTHUR HERTZBERG is Professor of Religion at Dartmouth College and Adjunct Professor of History at Columbia University. He is the author most recently of *The Jews in America: Four Centuries of an Uneasy Encounter,* New York, 1989.

MARTHA HIMMELFARB is Associate Professor of Religion at Princeton University. She is the author of *Tours of Hell: An Apocalyptic Form in Jewish and Christian Literature* (Philadelphia, 1983) and has recently completed a study of ascent to heaven in Jewish and Christian apocalypses.

EDWARD A. SYNAN is prelate of honor, F.R.S.C., Professor, Mediaeval Philosophy, Pontifical Institute of Mediaeval Studies at the University of Toronto 1959—; President of the Pontifical Institute 1973–1979; Acting President, January 1989–July 1990. Publications: *The Popes and the Jews in the Middle Ages* (1965); *The Works of Richard of Campsall,* 2 Vols. (1972, 1983); "St. Thomas Aquinas and the Profession of Arms," *Mediaeval Studies* 50 (1988) 404–437.

Index

Clemens Thoma and Michael Wyschogrod, editors, *Parable and Story in Judaism and Christianity* (A Stimulus Book, 1989).

Eugene J. Fisher and Leon Klenicki, editors, *In Our Time: The Flowering of Jewish-Catholic Dialogue* (A Stimulus Book, 1990).

Leon Klenicki, editor, *Toward a Theological Encounter* (A Stimulus Book, 1991).

David Burrell and Yehezkel Landau, editors, *Voices from Jerusalem* (A Stimulus Book, 1992).

John Rousmaniere, *A Bridge to Dialogue: The Story of Jewish-Christian Relations* (A Stimulus Book, 1991).

Michael E. Lodahl, *Shekhinah/Spirit: Divine Presence in Jewish and Christian Religion* (A Stimulus Book, 1992).

George M. Smiga, *Pain and Polemic: Anti-Judaism in the Gospels* (A Stimulus Book, 1992).

STIMULUS BOOKS are developed by Stimulus Foundation, a not-for-profit organization, and are published by Paulist Press. The Foundation wishes to further the publication of scholarly books on Jewish and Christian topics that are of importance to Judaism and Christianity.

Stimulus Foundation was established by an erstwhile refugee from Nazi Germany who intends to contribute with these publications to the improvement of communication between Jews and Christians.

Books for publication in this Series will be selected by a committee of the Foundation, and offers of manuscripts and works in progress should be addressed to:

Stimulus Foundation
785 West End Ave.
New York, N.Y. 10025